MW00985904

Living and Writing on the Coast of Maine

Thoughts on Life, Love, and Writing

Lea Wait

author of the Shadows Antique Print Mystery Series, the
Mainely Needlepoint Mystery Series, and five historical novels

copyright @2015 by Lea Wait
ISBN: 978-0-9964084-2-4

Contents

Part II - Writing and The Writing Life

Living and Loving on the Coast of Maine

Celebrating October 28:
A Love Story

My husband, Bob Thomas, and I have been married twelve years. Practically newlyweds, considering our (sh!) ages. But, of course, there's a story behind every marriage. Our story began April 1, 1968. (Yes. April Fools' Day.)

We were both young college graduates working in the same office in lower Manhattan a block from where the World Trade Center was being built. I came from Maine and New Jersey. Bob was born in the Bronx but grew up in Beirut, Lebanon, where his father's office was. (He often says if you were born anywhere in the United States in the twentieth or twenty-first centuries, you've used up all the luck a person deserves. He's seen refugee camps.)

We both loved talking about politics and books over wine and cheese. He was recently married. We became friends as well as colleagues.

Three years later he took the photographs at my wedding.

Mine was a short-lived marriage, and, as it turned out, so was his. After both our marriages were over, we fell in

3

love. Maybe we'd loved each other before that.

But our dreams weren't headed in the same direction. I'd decided to adopt children, and my job tied me to the New York/New Jersey area. Soon my mother moved in with me for a few months each year. And then longer. She and Bob didn't get along.

Bob was restless; he accepted jobs in zip codes far and wide. He got to know my growing family when his work took him to New York. He'd stay a year or two, but then leave, off on another job; another possibility. We loved each other, but we didn't love the lives the other had chosen.

My four daughters grew up. By the time they were out of high school, Bob and I weren't in touch. I continued caring for my mother. I left corporate life, moved to Maine, and began writing full-time, as I'd always dreamed I would.

I didn't know Bob had left his job to care for his mother. After she died of pancreatic cancer he married. In a horrible irony, two months after his mother's death his wife was also diagnosed with pancreatic cancer. She died seven months later.

Two years later, a short email: "Where are you? How are you? Thinking about you," brought us together again.

Six months later my mother died. A year after that Bob and I went quietly to the Town Hall in Wiscasset, Maine, and were married. It was 12,994 days after we'd first met.

Now Bob is painting. I'm writing. We both love living in Maine and being grandparents. We still talk politics and books over wine and cheese. Finally, our dreams have taken us down the same path.

Happy anniversary, my dearest husband. You, and this life we've made together, were worth waiting for.

Where I Come From

I live on the coast of Maine.

For most people that statement conjures up visions of lighthouses and lobsters and moose and breakers hitting high rocky shores. And those pictures are indeed part of "my" Maine.

It's hard to live in Maine during the summer and avoid signs for "Best Lobstah Rolls - Here!" and "Maine-ly Tee Shirts - Cheap!" and "Twenty-six miles to L.L. Bean!"

As most Mainers do, I wear several hats. One of my hats belongs to an antique print dealer. I've been one longer than Maggie Summers, my protagonist in the Shadows Antique Print Mystery series, has. So I also smile at the "Antiques, Used and New" signs, and the "Vintage Clothing" stores, and the "Auction! Here! Saturday night!" directional arrows. I even "Brake for Flea Markets" sometimes.

One of my hats is being an author. I write mysteries for adults and historical fiction for children aged eight and up. So my Maine includes visits to book festivals, libraries, book stores, schools, and historical society archives.

My husband is an artist. Art gallery openings and

museum exhibits and art supply stores are a regular part of our life together.

But Maine has been a part of me since I was in kindergarten. Long enough for me to know, yes, about lobster rolls and beaches and sunlight rocky shores. But also long enough to know about the folks who drink too much in their trailers, who depend on moose hunting to supply meat for the winter, who can't afford to heat their homes, whose teenagers drop out of school to dig for sea worms for a living or work as chambermaids, and who resent the rich folks with out of state license plates who seem to spend money so freely and then leave when it's time to board up for winter. Most Mainers work two or three jobs to survive. At least two of those jobs likely depend on the tourist industry.

Right now, early October, is, of course, leaf peeping season in the northeast. Vermont and Maine compete with each other to see who has the most spectacular foliage. (Admittedly, Vermont has the traditional reputation - but Maine has the wider variety of deciduous trees, and its number of fall tourists is growing yearly.) In Maine, this season is known (quietly) by the locals as the time when the "newly wed and nearly dead" visit. Said with a wry smile. These tourists are folks without children, and often with money. Quieter types than the "summer complaints," to be sure. The sort that enjoy art galleries and high-end restaurants and auctions and drives along the shore, and probably will pick up some holiday gifts for the family at craft and antique shops along the way. (Love those folks from away!)

Meanwhile those of us who live here year 'round are preparing for winter. My husband's ordered extra canvases, and other supplies artists in warmer climes might not think of: bio bricks and cords of word to heat the woodstove in his studio.

I'm finishing up my Christmas shopping so I won't have to think about going out later this year when weather might be complicated, and I'll be deep into writing my next book.

Because winter, at least at our house, means hunkering down and focusing on new work. We have neighbors who are cabinetmakers and quilt makers. At our house we work on books and canvases. We enjoy wine and cheese and conversations with friends occasionally. We bake bread or cookies or meatloaf or make stew when the muses are playing hooky. We catch up with movies and books we were too busy to read or see during the summer.

Winter in Maine also means buying Christmas wreaths by the side of the road (they're so inexpensive some people hang them in almost every window,) eating tiny freshly-caught shrimp in season, laying in a supply of birdseed for heavy snowfalls, and seeing spectacular sunsets reflected in the snow and ice on the edges of the rivers.

I've never understood why some people leave Maine and go south for the winter. But it does leave more space here for the rest of us.

I Ought To …

It's October. I know, because I can see orange leaves on trees outside my study window. I'd really love to go for a long walk and breathe in the crisp air before the temperatures drop below freezing.

But I ought to start sorting through the Christmas gifts I buy all year 'round, start wrapping, make lists, and see if I need anything else for my children or their children. I should go through the stack of cartons I save in case I need to ship something, and pick out those I'll be using for Christmas. The others can go in the barn, on their way to the recycling center.

I ought to take a pile of summer clothes to the cleaner's, and move my winter slacks and jackets from their summer homes into my closet. Before temperatures drop I really need to sew on all the buttons that fell off my flannel shirts last winter. I'm pretty sure I saved them all in a corner of my jewelry box. Which reminds me, I need to clean my jewelry, especially the silver pieces. Tarnish is damaging.

I should call the propane company to make sure our generator is set for winter. And order some kiln-dried wood and bio bricks for the wood stove in my husband's studio. But before that I need to clean out the barn, so there's space for the wood and the bricks. That means taking old magazines, newspapers and cardboard to the recycling center. All those bottles in the barn need to go to the redemption center. Every five cents helps. Plus, we need space for the bottles we'll empty during the winter. I should check to see when I'll be near New Hampshire in the near future, where liquor and wine are less expensive than in Maine. If I make a list of all the libations we'll need for the holidays, I can get them in the house and save a few dollars.

I should start bringing the porch furniture into the barn. And cover the porch cushions and put them away, too. I'd better not forget to turn off the outside water before that pipe freezes and breaks. And after I do that I should drain the garden hose and hang it in the barn, ready for next year.

Our mosquito magnet is still out, and the mosquitos are finally gone, so the mosquito magnet should be cleaned and put away for the winter. Which reminds me. The mosquitos and black flies may be gone, but it's about time for the mice to arrive.

I don't mind sharing our cellar or barn with them during the winter, but there are electric wires on the second floor of the ell and in the attic. Traps or poison. Must get some.

I have a pile of books to donate to the library. The lamp next to my husband's bed really should be repaired.

And I've been meaning to stop at the jewelry store to see if any of my watches can be repaired, or whether I'll have to continue carrying a travel alarm clock around in my pocketbook.

I should clean the bird feeders before it gets too cold. And put away the bird bath. Oh, and I should really get some of those stakes with reflectors on them to put at the end of the driveway so people – especially people plowing our driveway – don't plow our lawn instead.

Which reminds me. I'd better call the guy who plowed our driveway last year to make sure we're on his list for this year. I should put down all the storm windows, and put balsam-filled "snakes" on all the window sills and where the top and bottom windows meet. (I could find out what that place is called, while I'm at it.) I should close off the rooms we don't use (and therefore don't heat) in the winter, and block their doorways with blankets or more snakes.

I'd better check the outside lights. Replacing bulbs in ice and snow isn't fun.

Oh, and I need to do some writing, too. Get a good start on the three books I have deadlines for next year.

But before that, I should order postcards and bookmarks for my book that will be out in January. (That means I'll need a lot of labels and stamps. I should put them on my list. And stamps for the Christmas cards I should be looking for this time of year.)

I need to find something to wear (I should have gone on a diet, but it's a little late for that) to my high school reunion this coming weekend, and to my nephew's wedding in Phoenix in November, and to the children's book festival and signings and library talks I agreed to do back in July, when November and December seemed a long time away, and promoting a Christmas mystery and a book for children at the end of the year made sense. (Did I really schedule three events in two states within a day and a half? Do they need posters or an author bio or bookmarks to promote the events? Have I confirmed all the details?)

I should read the new books just published by my fellow Maine Crime Writers.

I've had my flu shot, but I should take the cat to the vet for a checkup. Maybe she needs one. I've never had a cat before, so I don't want to make a mistake with her.

First, though, I think I'll write all these things down. If they're on a list, I won't forget them. And it will be fun to cross them out. A list is a good idea.

I think I'll start it right after I take that walk.

Me and My Encyclopedias

I grew up in a family of antique dealers. As a child my summer Saturday mornings were spent in Round Pond, Maine, attending outdoor country auctions run by Robert Foster, father of the Robert Foster who holds auctions in Newcastle, Maine, today.

My grandmother was a doll and toy dealer (like Gussie White in my *Shadows* series.) My mother was looking for furniture and colonial fireplace equipment for our home. I was fascinated by the people and the antiques and the auctioneer. I longed to be brave enough to raise my hand; to bid, like the grownups surrounding me, sitting on folding chairs on that uneven lawn overlooking Round Pond Harbor.

Every week I carefully examined all the items to be sold. While prospective buyers took notes, planning possible purchases, I fantasized about what I would purchase if I could. Two things stood in my eleven-year-old way. Courage. And funds. My allowance was small. I seldom had more than a dollar or two in my pocket. Most items at that auction, even back in those "old days," went for a good deal more than that.

Until one July day. It was steaming hot. Not many people had shown up, and those who had brought umbrellas or large hats to shade them. Mr. Foster's children were selling cold bottles of Moxie and Coke out of a cooler when one of the runners brought up two large boxes full of old books. Foster held one volume up and had the runner tip a box so potential buyers could see the rest.

"Here we have enough reading for the rest of the year. A really old encyclopedia. Guaranteed to be totally out of date. Who wants it?" No one said anything. Then he said the magic words. "Who'll give me one dollar for the lot?"

And I raised my hand.

He grinned and pointed at me, not even looking for another bid. "Sold! To the young lady for one dollar!" The runner brought the boxes over and dropped them on the ground next to me.

I was in heaven.

My grandmother looked at me and smiled, shaking her head. "Now, why'd you buy those books?" she asked.

"Because some day I'm going to write historical novels," I told her, making up an answer on the spot. "They'll be good for research." (I must have sounded very pompous.)

She just nodded. And she shared my excitement when, in true antique dealer fashion, we examined the books, did some research and realized I'd just bought a complete, mint, first edition of the *Encyclopedia Americana* (1829-1833,) with many uncut pages.

It's stayed with me ever since, and is in my study today.

Last month that *Americana* was joined, courtesy of my writing friend Sherie Schmauder, who was blessed with two full copies, by the twenty nine volumes of the eleventh edition (1910-1911) of the *Encyclopedia Britannica*. That edition is another very special one. As with my *Americana*, some information in it may not be correct today. But the eleventh edition of the *Britannica* includes nineteenth century data and political and social views on a myriad of issues that are hard to find anywhere else. It was assembled while the *Britannica* was in transition from its British publisher to its American publisher, so it includes articles by experts from two continents.

I look forward to exploring it, and using it when I write my next historical novel. Reference books of the period are a wonderful way to put you back in the days of your characters.

Nothing can replace touching and reading the pages my characters might have looked at, one or two hundred years ago.

Addicted to Politics

I could measure my life by elections.

My family bought their first television set to watch the 1956 political conventions. I lay on my stomach on the floor of our family room in New Jersey, my eyes fixed on the small black and white screen, fascinated by the banners and voting.

In early 1960 my grandmother took me to Washington. She was trying to get a passport so she could visit to Scotland, where she had relatives, and where she'd spent time as a child, but all proofs of where she'd been born had been destroyed in a Boston fire. She was sadly unsuccessful in her quest for a passport, but I fell in love with Washington.

I remember every minute of that trip, but two places stand out. First, the National Archives. Seeing the actual documents I'd read about in history classes, with the real signatures. Not just the Declaration and the Constitution, but (okay, I was a seventh-grade geek,) I remember standing in awe in front of the actual Gadsden Purchase.

But the highlight of the trip was sitting above the Senate Chamber, seeing it in action. Senators Bartlett and

Gruening from the new state of Alaska were presenting a bill. No; I don't remember what it was for. But I decided at that moment that someday I wanted to work in Washington; maybe even be a senator.

That summer I watched the 1960 convention sitting on the floor in the house we owned in Maine — the same home I live in today. I begged to stay up as late as it was on. The Democratic convention was one of the most exciting conventions ever — votes and more votes. Compromises and negotiations. I loved the roll calls and kept my own tallies. My parents and grandparents were Republicans, but that didn't matter. I loved the theatre of it all.

It was after that convention that I began collecting political memorabilia — buttons, tickets to conventions and inaugurations and impeachments, signatures, and other campaign miscellanea from the nineteenth and twentieth centuries. (I sold my collection only a couple of years ago.)

I wasn't as active in politics as many Baby Boomers were — but the Civil Rights, Peace, and Women's Rights movements of the sixties and early seventies were the background of my life, as they were for many people my age. As I think back, I wish I'd done more. In high school, I had a friend whose family actively supported South and Central American revolutionaries, and I met many of them. (I often wonder exactly who they were. I was trusted to know where they were from, and in some cases what they were doing, but was never told their names.)

I was involved in a lot of late-night discussions. I took part in demonstrations for causes I believed in. I handed out leaflets at a steel mill in Pittsburgh, where I went to college. I registered to vote as soon as I was 21 so I could vote for George McGovern in the Democratic primary. After college I joined the Village Independent Democrats in New York City, passed out more leaflets, and stuffed envelopes. Many of my friends were Vietnam Veterans Against the War, but most of them wore suits to work. We weren't on the fringes of society. We were going to change it from within.

At least that was the plan.

One of my high school friends' sister was on the FBI's "most wanted list" (for actions related to Civil Rights issues) for a while and neighbors in Greenwich Village told me I was being investigated by the FBI. They, and I, considered that an honor.

It was that kind of time.

Sometimes working within the system made a difference. I was thrilled when a speech I wrote started Bell System retirees' reaching out to poor, predominantly African-American, areas, and tutoring in schools.

More often, the system didn't work. Or worked too slowly to make a real difference. But I never missed voting in a presidential or mid-term election.

When I had children I took them with me to the polls, to show them how important it was. Now that I work at home, my husband jokes that CNN is our best friend. We watch it for a couple of hours each day. Sometimes (yes,

I'm confessing) more.

When I moved to Maine full-time, one of my first steps was to go to our Town Hall to register to vote. The town clerk, a neighbor, informed me, with a smile, that I didn't need to worry about registering early — I could register on Election Day. "Just come on in. We'll get you registered, Lea," she said. "No problem."

Used to states where you had to register at least six weeks in advance of an election, I insisted on registering early anyway. When I went to vote in Maine for the first time I was secretly delighted to find that, as usual, Maine did it their way. For the first time in my life I was handed a paper ballot and a pencil. After I'd marked the paper I was instructed to fold it and put it in the large wooden box on the table in the center of the room. The same box they'd used for over a hundred years. After the polls closed, the box would be opened, and the votes counted by hand and the totals called in.

Four years ago my husband was one of those who counted the ballots. Tonight our next door neighbor will be taking a turn. Then he'll be joining his wife and daughter and another couple at our house to await the returns from the rest of the country.

Here in Maine we're voting for a senator, with an independent candidate a strong contender running against Republican and Democratic candidates. We have a ballot issue on approving same sex marriage. We have local elections. And, above all, there's the presidency.

Of course, I have strong opinions about each of those

decisions.

Not all of us waiting in my living room tonight will have voted the same way.

But we'll talk, and nosh, and have a few drinks. I predict more than a few, if the night grows long. Some of us will no doubt end the evening happier than others. But we'll still be friends tomorrow. And the world — and the United States – and the State of Maine – will continue.

After all. There's a mid-term election in only two years. Another presidential election in four. We always have another chance. That's one of the wonderful things about our country.

Merry Christmas from Maine

Those romantic winter wonderland Christmas cards with scenes of snow-covered roads and pine trees and white colonial homes with wreathed doors, horses and sleighs, snowmen, heavily laden Christmas trees, towns with candles in every window, town carolers... all those pictures that come to our collective American minds .... tend to be reminiscent of Currier & Ives scenes from the mid-1800s winter in New England.

This year I'll be spending my sixteenth Christmas in Maine. But most of my Christmases have been spent further south — in New York, or New Jersey, or even further away from Maine. In states where my children and their families live, work, and go to school.

My first Maine Christmas is very clear in my memory. It was 1975. My mother had retired north, and that year somehow the whole family managed to gather in Maine to celebrate together.

I was living in Greenwich Village then, working in lower Manhattan during the day, and attending New York University full-time at night to earn graduate degrees. I was in my late twenties; I'd been married and divorced, and had decided I wanted to adopt one or more children. Friday nights I volunteered with abused children between the ages of six and twelve at the New York Foundling Hospital, and my application at a New York City adoption agency was complete. Bob, my boyfriend at the time (the guy who only 28 years later became my husband) had taken the pictures for my home study.

His family was living in Caracas, Venezuela that year (his father worked for a multi-national company,) so I suggested he spend the holidays with my family. He couldn't resist the idea of a romantic Maine Christmas, so we agreed to rent a car and head north.

Bob picked me up at my Christopher Street apartment a little after noon Christmas Eve, since I had to work that morning. Three blocks into our trip he turned to me and asked, "Do you think I'll need gloves in Maine?" I assured him he would. We double-parked while he ran into a drugstore and bought a pair.

It started to snow by the time we reached Connecticut. By Massachusetts the snow was several inches deep. By Maine, it was a classic winter wonderland.

We didn't spend another Christmas in Maine together until almost twenty-five years later.

Most of those other years I spent with my daughters (and sometimes with Bob) in New Jersey.

Christmas was always my favorite time of the year.

For many years I had (among other collections) many, many Santa Clauses. My daughters and I would start decorating on the Saturday or Sunday after Thanksgiving.

The Santas would be unpacked to appear on the mantel, on table tops, and on walls.

We always had two Christmas trees — one large, real, one that would go up and be decorated a day or two before Christmas, and one small tree, hung with tiny ornaments, that was artificial, and would go up when the Santas did. And because my daughters were born in Asia, we had a wreath hung with ornaments from their countries: Thailand, Korea, Hong Kong and India.

Each year I hosted a large party (150-200 people) on the first Sunday in December for single adoptive parents, their children, and prospective single parents. The first prospective single dad who arrived received the honor of being ushered upstairs to don the Santa suit I had waiting.

Many years later I ran into a woman who'd been one of my young guests. She told me that for years she'd believed Santa lived at my house.

The adoptive parent party would be followed by a luncheon for those in my corporate work department at AT&T, and finally, by a special Christmas Eve party for family and close friends.

Today, instead of hosting family and extended family and friends, I spend Christmas with Bob, who, I'll admit, is a bit of a Grinch. No, the holidays aren't the same. Although I love being with him, I miss the excitement and joy of past Christmases.

I've even divested some of the Santas. But I still have that small artificial tree. Forty-five years ago it was the top of an artificial tree used as a prop in a Christmas safety film I produced. It was first decorated in my single-gal apartment in Greenwich Village.

And I still hang stockings on the mantelpiece, treasure every Christmas card that comes to remind me of family and friends not in Maine, and plan special food for the holidays.

Life changes. But I still love Christmas, even toned down. I look for gifts for children and grandchildren all year, and love wrapping them up and sending them, imagining how they'll be received. I love the special food we have Christmas morning (filet mignon and mushrooms and champagne). I love Christmas carols and sappy Christmas movies and the Christmas cards and packages that arrive at our door, reminding us of loved ones celebrating in other places.

I loved writing my latest Shadows mystery (*Shadows on a Maine Christmas*) because it felt as though I was celebrating with Maggie and Will and Aunt Nettie. I even gave them my special Christmas breakfast.

And, now that I'm a writer, I also have the joy of knowing that, through my books, I'll be under many Christmas trees this year.

That makes me very happy.

Cooking Our Christmas Goose

Bob and I live far from daughters, brothers, and sisters, so we spend our holidays cozily together in Maine, dependent on telephone calls, Skype visits, and email to tie us to family and friends. We've developed our own way of celebrating.

We both love cooking. And eating. (No doubt too much the second.) And careers as an artist and a writer aren't exercise conducive. So after the holidays, each year we become Spartan, and we diet. Atkins, usually, and usually for several months.

But before that, we have one last adventurous meal.

Last Christmas, we discussed our options for several weeks. (The decision is, of course, at least half the fun, especially if made while sipping wine and lingering over an assortment of tempting cookbooks.)

We decided to cook a goose.

Neither of us had ever done that before. And, after all, Christmas goose is traditional. Dickens, among other authorities, says so.

We knew just where such a perfect fowl could be obtained. On a small hill on Route 90 in Warren sits an enticing shop called Curtis Custom Meats. Although Curtis specializes in cuts of beef, lamb and pork (perhaps plebian elsewhere, but not here, where they butcher their own), Curtis Meats is also the place for obtaining chicken, turkey, quail, and duck. Goose? But of course.

I was doing a book signing in Camden, so I was the one appointed to pick out our goose. The day I was there they had half a dozen to choose from. I'd never bought a goose, so I was a bit dismayed by two facts.

First, geese are much longer and skinnier than the turkeys and chickens I was used to cooking. Second, they are MUCH more expensive. (Think $50 instead of $12 for a similarly sized turkey.) I'll admit I almost chickened out right then. But we'd decided on goose, so goose it was. I choose one and he (she?) came home with me.

The next step was pouring through cookbooks again. How to cook our goose?

Perhaps overly influenced by several viewings of *Julie and Julia*, we decided Julia Child would be our authority. She informed us we would first need to steam our duck in a covered roaster to render the fat.

We did not own a covered roaster.

So the weekend before the big "cooking of the goose" we headed for a kitchen supply store. The owner told us, kindly, that covered roasters hadn't been made in perhaps thirty years.

"But," we explained, "Julia said!"

"You could use foil," she suggested. Several other helpful customers chimed in with similar suggestions.

"Have any of you ever cooked a goose?" we asked. No one had.

In lieu of options, we decided foil would have to do, although it didn't fit Julia's strict instruction for a "tight cover."

Her next command was titled, "Surgery." I won't bore you with details other than to confirm that, yes, a goose contains a great deal of fat. I felt as though I'd applied about twenty layers of suet to every part of my body that came near that bird.

Surgery was followed by Seasoning. Trussing. Steaming. Braising. Roasting. And, finally – Browning. Gravy and Carving completed the operation.

The entire process took longer than Julia suggested, and required a great deal of checking along the way (which probably lengthened the cooking time, since we did more than the usual oven peeking and temperature taking.)

Julia also decreed that the only acceptable stuffing for a goose had to include prunes, so we made her prune and apple stuffing with sausage. We had our doubts about it in theory. But it turned out rich and spectacular.

Result? The goose was good, but, we sadly decided, for us not really worth the time and money we'd spent on it. (That stuffing was fantastic, though!)

We saved the goose fat and liver for other experiments, other days, so considered those bonuses.

And – we do recommend goose for the holidays. Or – for one holiday, anyway. It was fun.

For New Year's we had filet mignon smothered in

mushrooms and a goose liver and port pate´. (Hmmm ….
wonder where that liver came from ???!) Served with
champagne, of course. We believe champagne goes with
everything. We're very flexible when it comes to
champagne.

On to a New Year. And a new diet.

New Year's Eve Fantasies

New Year's Eve! The yearly chance to symbolically wipe the slate clean and begin a new year, full of unknown joys, sorrows, adventures, achievements, and memories.

Throughout the world each new year is celebrated with parties, fireworks, prayers, jubilation, and resolutions; with tearing up the old and beginning the new; and with popping corks and dreams, perhaps this year to finally be fulfilled.

The earliest New Year's Eves I remember were spent with my grandparents, watching Guy Lombardo on television, seeing the ball drop in Times Square, eating Christmas cookies, and sipping ginger ale before I was shooed upstairs to bed. As I grew older I begged for champagne, which I finally was allowed when I was about fifteen. I was dreadfully disappointed when the kind my grandparents shared tasted more or less like stale ginger ale.

I dreamed of New Year's Eves like the ones in Fred Astaire and Ginger Rogers movies. I was sure when I was grown up I would celebrate New Year's Eves the way Fred and Ginger did in their movies.

Years went by, Guy Lombardo's band was in color instead of black and white, and Dick Clark took over the midnight gig. But my New Year's Eves didn't change much. I grew up and moved to New York's Greenwich Village, but, sadly, my life didn't become Fred and Ginger's.

The world had changed. At one New Year's party in the Village I was not only the only one not wearing jeans, I strongly suspected I was the only one who'd arrived sober. Trying to fit in, I had a glass (or two) of punch (equal parts vodka, champagne, and white wine,) but after a couple of hours of watching people passing out on the floor, smoking hash, or throwing up, I went home, watched the ball drop forty blocks north, and wrote doleful poetry.

A few years later I moved to the Jersey suburbs, where I was single, couples gave parties for other couples, and I watched the ball drop and served ginger ale to my children.

One year a friend still in the city suggested I join him: we'd have dinner and then go to Times Square to watch the Big Event in person. Finally, a New Year's adventure! I arrived to find he'd decided that, for auld lang syne, that afternoon he'd telephoned his high school girl friend of twenty years before to tell her he still loved her. She'd told him to get lost.

Yes, we went to Times Square. (It was crowded and crazy, as expected.)

He spent the rest of the night drinking and crying for

his lost love. I would have gone home to Jersey, but buses had stopped running by the time he'd sobered up enough that I was convinced he really wasn't going to kill himself in his high school sweetheart's honor.

Memorable evening? No doubt. But not memories I'd cherish.

The closest I got to a theoretically glamorous New Year's Eve was the year I spent midnight on a hotel rooftop in Tuscany, drinking wine and watching *Singing in the Rain* (in Italian, of course) with two dozen other parents of teenagers attending a special school there. I'll admit the town's fireworks were lovely, and I wrote a lot in my journal that night. But, bottom line, it was one more New Year's Eve alone. I was the only single parent in a crowd of couples clinging to each other and wishing they were home in Santa Barbara.

That year I pretty much decided New Year's Eve was Fred and Ginger's night. Not mine.

And then, twelve years ago, I got married. And ten years ago my husband and I were wandering the streets of old Quebec City in the early fall and happened upon a restaurant called Le Saint-Amour. The menu sounded enticing, so we made a reservation for that night. And went back two nights later. And made a reservation for three months later, for New Year's Eve.

And, yes, it was magic.

Fred and Ginger wouldn't have been able to dance. But they could have worn their most elegant clothes. And the nine small courses, all chosen by the chef and served with paired wines by gentlemen in tuxedoes in a glassed in room lit with tiny white lights, with snow falling above and music playing, were perfect.

The evening was a flawlessly performed drama. The food was displayed to perfection, and the delicious courses, which started at eight in the evening, were timed precisely so that the final presentation, a selection of hand-dipped chocolates served with champagne, arrived at exactly midnight, as the elegant waiters handed each guest a noisemaker and the musicians played Auld Lang Syne.

The women put on their fur coats and gloves and gentlemen bundled up in hats and scarves and boots and everyone went out onto the snow-covered streets lit by thousands of white lights. It was snowing lightly. Once in a while a horse-drawn carriage clopped by. We walked the several blocks back to our grand old hotel in the heart of Old Quebec, passing others dressed in everything from formal attire to ski jackets, all smiling and wishing everyone else a "Bonne année!"

Now I know what New Year's Eve can be.

Hoping yours this year is exactly the way you dream it will be.

Cold Days

Our house was built in 1774 on an island in the tidal Sheepscot River.

It has six fireplaces, which were the only heat sources in the house (other than one space heater) until my parents had a furnace installed in 1974. Classically for New England, the dooryard faces south, to get as much warmth as possible, and the fewest windows are on the north side.

This winter has been an especially challenging one for those of us who choose to make Maine our home. Normally we have between twenty-five and forty inches of snow by this time in the area where I live, near the coast. This winter we've had almost eighty inches in the past month.

As I write this the snow is falling again. The next storm is due in a couple of days. And – did I mention? For the past month the temperatures have been in single digits or below at night. Some warm days they've risen to the teens during the day.

But, considering it all, few people really complain. After all, we chose to live here. And this is an unusually snowy and cold winter.

Plus, this is 2015. Most people have some form of central heat. Storm windows. Insulation. Grocery stores. Running water. Stoves. Silk or thermal underwear. Fleece. Flannel. Wool. Plows. Salt and sand. And heated cars or trucks to get us from one heated place to another on plowed roads.

For hundreds – perhaps thousands – of years, people survived here without those things.

I'm not an expert on the ways Abenakis and Micmacs survived winters.

But I do know a little about how Europeans lived here at the time my home was built. When the river wasn't just patchworked with ice floes … it was frozen hard enough so people used it for sleigh races.

People prepared all year for winter. In snowy months men took sledges into the woods and lumbered. Wood was chopped in summer so it would be dry for winter fireplaces. Fires were kept burning day and night. Warmly dressed people slept two to four to a bed or pallet near the fire.

Pine boughs were woven together in fall and piled around a house's foundation. Snow filled the gaps, helping insulate the building. Melted snow served for occasional washing, and for the soups and stews that, with bread, were sustenance. Fish, meat, vegetables and fruit were harvested in summer and dried or smoked, to be resurrected in winter. Clothes weren't washed for months. Even infant's clouts (diapers) were hung to dry in kitchens with little rinsing.

In Maine, small workrooms (the ell) connected houses to their barns, so animals could be fed without going outside. Privies were often located in the far corner of the barn. Roads were not plowed. Sleighs pulled heavy pieces of wood to push deep snow down so horses and sleighs didn't sink in it.

Most people stayed home for the winter. "Winter well!" was a common farewell in fall. Those who didn't live in town might not see neighbors until spring. Babies would be born, people would die, and no one outside the family would know for months. Sometimes a whole family would die, of disease or hunger or cold or fire or depression that led to violence, and no one would know until late spring, when muddy roads dried and were again passable.

Today only two of the six fireplaces in my home can be used. One flue is lined and connected to the furnace, and one flue and chimney is for the wood stove in my husband's studio. Maybe someday we'll be able to afford to bring the others "up to code" so they'll be safe to use.

In the meantime our furnace and woodstove do fine, even considering that temperatures have been in the single digits (and below) for the past couple of weeks.

But the low temperatures make me think about the families who lived here two hundred years ago.

No global warming broke bitter temperatures then. The wide river across the street from our home, on which there are ice floes today, then froze solid. Snow fell more often, and lasted longer. Occupants of this house were lucky: it had glass windows — luxury items in 1774, probably imported from England. To protect rooms from winds off the river, all most folks could do was close their shutters. But then they'd also close off the light.

About 1840, when Captain Enoch Chase bought this house, he was a widower with eight children. He'd just married again, a young woman named Sarah, who in her time gave birth to six children. At one time, according to the local census, nineteen people lived in this house, including two young women and one man who "helped out."

Their house had five bedrooms, and, of course, no indoor bathrooms.

On cold days, as I walk through these rooms, which I now share only with my husband, I think of Enoch and Sarah and their children. I wonder who slept where, and which room was set aside for spinning and weaving. And which daughter (I'm sure there was at least one) scorched her skirt by standing too close to one of the fires.

I think of Sarah, giving birth in this house. And of her (and Enoch and several of their children) dying here. I wonder what they thought of the Civil War. None of their sons enlisted, but most were at sea then, on clipper ships in the Pacific. One died there.

I write historical novels for children, and Sarah's grandmother, who lived in this house in the late eighteenth and early nineteenth century, is in one of my books (Sally Clough, in *Stopping to Home*,) and one of her uncles (Rev. Jonathan Adams) is in my *Wintering Well*.

I didn't know any of them, but their footsteps are still here, and I think of them.

And on days like this, when the temperature is near zero, I wonder. How did they stay warm? And often I turn my thermostat down a degree or two. We keep it at sixty during the day.

Sarah and Enoch would have laughed at our being such wimps.

But I suspect they would have envied us, too.

And I thank them. They, and others like them in other parts of our country, were survivors. And so our new country survived.

A little snow and cold? Just part of life.

Tea and Me

I drink tea. That's right. No coffee. No soda (although the protagonist in my Shadows Antique Mystery series is devoted to her Diet Pepsi).

I probably inherited my love of tea from my grandmother. A Scot from Edinburgh through and through, despite the fact that she'd been born in Boston in 1890, her life had taken her back and forth to "the auld country" often as a child. For her, no afternoon was complete without tea. It didn't necessarily have to include shortbread or scones, but sometimes it did. And since my grandparents lived with my parents and sisters and I for most of my childhood, I have warm memories of coming home from school and enjoying a cup of hot tea (with milk and a teaspoonful of sugar) with my grandmother.

And we had wonderful tea. Every Christmas we would get an unmarked carton of tea bags from one of my grandmother's brothers. I was a teenager before I understood that this was, indeed, "special tea." I have no idea what kind of black tea it was. It was an unmarked private blend.

You see, that great-uncle who sent us the tea each year

had (yes, I'm telling the truth) invented the tea bag. Somewhere in my family files I have a copy of the patent, which I believe was dated in the 1930s. His name was William Patterson, should you want to check it out. Uncle Bill had sold his patent to Lipton, who, as part of the deal, agreed to send him select tea each year for the rest of his life.

That annual tea supply in my house ended when my grandmother died, but Uncle Bill lived to be ninety-eight. That's a lot of tea bags.

In high school, sitting on the floor in candle-lit darkness and listening to Bob Dylan with my friends, we all drank black coffee. But I sipped it slowly and suffered shortly after from stomach pains. It was hard to be a rebel when you didn't drink coffee, though, so I kept trying.

By the time I got to college I was a bit smarter, and had officially given up coffee experimentation. My drink was tea, although I hated the taste of the water where I went to school, so I added Diet Pepsi to my list of approved drinks for those four years.

When I started working at a corporation, coffee, again, was the politically acceptable drink. Water (hot or cold) or tea had not yet appeared in conference rooms. It was coffee or nothing. I was already obvious enough (I was usually the only woman in the room) so I filled my cup with plain water or milk, if it was available, and at meeting breaks ("coffee breaks," of course) I'd head to the company cafeteria where they did have tea.

By the time I left corporate life, thirty years later, tea

was always available at conferences and meetings, although there still weren't too many of us drinking it. Usually the carafe of hot water was unmarked, so the biggest danger was putting a tea bag in a cup and then pouring hot coffee on top of it.

Most recently, when I was at a mystery conference last fall, I did that again. A fellow tea drinker watched, sympathized, and offered to share his tea bag with me. (They were running low.) A truly generous soul! But now I carry my own. Just in case.

Today, sitting in my study in Maine, I've expanded my tea preferences. I begin my day with a cup of blueberry green tea, with added lemon juice. (For a couple of years I only drank green tea. Perhaps virtuous, but, especially in winter, I missed black tea.) Now my noon cup may either be green or black. Perhaps Earl Gray. Mid-afternoon calls for caffeine, so that cup is definitely black tea. But any caffeine after 4 p.m. ensures that I won't sleep well that night, so after then I move to herb teas.

Chamomile when I'm trying to relax. Red or Lemon Zinger if I'm still working. Or maybe another cup of green tea.

In the summer I brew my own iced tea: a mixture of black and herb teas. And on a very cold winter's afternoon, I've been known to add a touch of brandy to my mid-afternoon black tea.

Today others have discovered the joys of tea, and any supermarket has diverse and wonderful selections. Happily, studies have also shown that teas of all kinds have varying amounts of anti-oxidants, and might even help in weight loss. A nice thought.

I haven't noticed any major differences. But, then, tea has always been a part of my life.

I suspect it always will be.

Fannie Farmer Ruled Our Kitchen

Although I now live in Maine, and many of my books are set there, I'll admit that, technically, I am not a Mainer. I was born in Boston.

Boston, indeed, has been the hub of the maternal side of my family since 1889, the year my great-grandmother and grandfather arrived there from Edinburgh to begin their life together. My grandmother joined them, the requisite nine months later, in 1890.

Those first few years were busy – starting an import business, traveling back and forth to Ireland and Scotland, and managing to make my grandmother the oldest of seven in fairly regular fashion.

I don't know when Fannie Farmer's cookbooks joined the growing family, but my grandmother once told me her mother often referred to it for "American recipes." By that time, of course, my great-grandmother's cookbook was long worn out. My grandmother and mother had their own copies of later editions, one of which is now mine.

I grew up believing that if Fannie Farmer or Betty Crocker didn't know the answer about cooking, it wasn't worth knowing. But it wasn't until recently that I learned more about Fannie herself.

Born in 1857, she'd suffered a stroke in her teens, and become seriously disabled. Finally, in her mid-twenties, she was able to walk again, although with a limp, and decided she wanted to attend the well-known Boston Cooking School. She graduated when she was 32, and was asked to remain there as a supervisor, and, eventually, as the director of the school. It was then that she wrote the book she's remembered for: *The Boston Cooking-School Cook Book*, known almost universally as "Fannie Farmer."

Her publisher, Little Brown, initially turned the book down, so in 1896 Farmer suggested she herself would pay for the first printing of 3,000 copies. They sold, and Little Brown didn't hesitate again.

They made the right decision. Since then the cookbook has gone through many editions, and has sold nearly four million copies. (Farmer's heirs still retain the copyright.)

My 1942 edition of the *Cook Book* includes thirty-seven chapters devoted to subjects from menus and beverages to cheeses, garnishes, sauces, poultry and game (including pigeons), confections, pickles, and frozen desserts. At the beginning is a list of "Fifty Basic Recipes for Students and Beginners" which starts with "white bread," and goes on to include "brown stock," "mayonnaise," "soft custard," "French soufflé," "puff pastry", "petits fours," and "jelly."

Fannie had high expectations for her cooks.

Many of my family's traditional Christmas cookies and puddings come straight from Fannie Farmer, and if I have any doubt about a recipe I remember my mother or grandmother making, I go straight to the book I know may be the source. She seldom fails me.

Thank you, Fannie Farmer, for being a part of my family's life for more than three generations.

Thoughts on Valentine's Day

I've been trying to think of something to write about today.

Bartlett's Quotations lists no memorable words under the heading "Valentine's Day." I know, because I just checked. But this is a day to write something sentimental and witty and bright. The day for lovers.

I know the history. Although there were several St. Valentines, the one usually thought of at this time of year was the Christian imprisoned for performing wedding ceremonies for soldiers in the Roman army who were forbidden to marry.

During the Middle Ages Valentine's Day became associated with romantic, courtly, love, and by the fifteenth century people were sending poetry, flowers, and sweets to "their Valentines." (And you thought it was just a Hallmark conspiracy!)

I'm currently reading a biography of Emily Dickinson (*My Wars Are Laid Away in Books*, by Alfred Habegger), and, sure enough, even young Emily wrote Valentine poems and sent them to men in Amherst. (There's no record of how many, if any, valentines she received in return.)

My memories of Valentine's Days past include years of cutting out uneven red paper hearts and messily pasting them on white doilies for loved family members, most likely as classroom or Brownie projects. In elementary school there was always a large decorated classroom box in which classmates were to deposit their valentines for other students. On Valentine's Day, in years before candy was considered inappropriate, we would share a few candy hearts and maybe red-frosted cupcakes, and the cards would be distributed with great fanfare.

Some children gave cards (often anonymously) to everyone in the class, but some boys would only give cards to boys (girls? yuck!) and some girls gave only to girls. The most popular kids, of course, got the most cards. And, inevitably, some students got very few. Bottom line: it was a painful process.

And it set the stage for the rest of life's Valentine's Days, in which those lucky enough to be part of a committed couple could happily celebrate or not, as they chose (and flaunt it, as some inevitably did) while those in early stages of relationships would nervously wonder what to do. (What would be too much? too little?) And those without a "significant other" would be forced to endure weeks of advertising about love and flowers and chocolate and feel unclaimed and unwanted.

Not even mentioning those who were part of a couple and somehow, despite the advertising deluge … oh, the horror of it! the guilt! Forgot Valentine's Day!

As an unmarried woman for most of my life, I knew

other single women who sent flowers to their own offices on Valentine's Day. And more who bought their favorite chocolates and stayed home and watched romantic movies alone, or with other singles, vowing this would definitely be the last year they would do such a thing.

One man I knew would always break up with his girl-of-the-season before Valentine's Day, to avoid "all that romantic crap."

The United States Greeting Card Association says about one hundred and ninety million individual valentines are sent every year. About half are sent to children. If you add the valentines made in school and the boxed varieties for those school exchanges, the number exchanged by students goes up to one billion. (Teachers, not surprisingly, get the most valentines.) Fifteen million e-Valentines were sent in 2010.

And, of course, you can buy valentines for your godmother or grandfather or your sister or brother-in-law … the greeting card industry has made sure you have no excuse for not finding a card for everyone in your life. (Not to speak of the flowers and candy and champagne and jewelry and restaurant industries, who'd like to help you out, too.)

And romantic love is very personal. It is magical; it is ephemeral; it is only part of the larger word "love." But those millions and billions of valentines are trying to encompass all of love. (I'm surprised there aren't valentines for dogs and cats and horses — or maybe I just haven't seen those.) That extremely broad interpretation of the word "love" is the commercial part of the holiday.

If you plan to have a quiet, romantic, dinner tonight with your partner, and celebrating this day means roses and jewelry and chocolate and dancing and a recommitment to your love … that's wonderful. You don't need it to be February 14 to make that happen, but if this date reminds you, or makes it more special in some way — have a wonderful day. I'm happy for you. Really I am.

For everyone else, happy or sad, in a relationship or not … my advice? Don't take February 14 too seriously. But do take advantage of this day in mid-February to remind yourself that spring will come soon. Buy yourself some spring flowers. Maybe even buy yourself a special dessert, or make something you love for dinner you haven't had recently.

Because you deserve it. And you don't need permission or a special day to do those things. February 14 is as good a day as any.

What are my husband and I going to do today? Well, we're having our cellar insulated, and we've been told we have to be out of the house for most of the day. Chances are good we'll visit an art museum, and probably have lunch somewhere. I'm looking forward to spending the day together outside the house; although we spend most days together inside the house, those are working days. Today, by the chance of the insulation folks' schedule, we'll be having a play day. Sounds perfect to me.

Happy Valentine's Day! May your day be perfect in its own way, too.

Comeuppance?

For the past couple of weeks I've been in bed. Not a romantic bed. Not a room-serviced bed (although my husband certainly gets multi-points for trying.)

Not even my own cozy bed.

I've been in exile in the guest room of our house, with germs, tissues, unending glasses of juice, and stacks of books and magazines I was too weak, for the most part, even to hold.

And, I'll have you know, this does not happen to me. I am tough. I almost never get a cold. I always have flu shots. I eat lots of vegetables. I've been taking assorted vitamins since I was twenty-five, varying them as studies indicated. I eat yogurt. I don't smoke.

All right, I do drink.

But I do not get sick — do you hear me??? Pain and illness are not things that stop me.

I was brought up that way. When I was growing up, fevers were tolerated for a day or maybe two, placated with bed rest, Campbell's Chicken Noodle Soup, tall glasses of iced ginger ale, and then — back to school with you! No germs dared linger long in our house.

When I was thirteen I first started getting serious monthly pains my mother called "that time." She considered any discussion of such indignities wimpish. Cramps were a fact of life to be coped with. When mine led to such embarrassments as fainting in school and being sent home, she was not pleased, and silently handed me a heating pad and an aspirin. (On the other hand, my grandmother, who lived with us, sometimes made me hot tea with a surreptitious bit of her private supply of cognac added in silent sympathy.)

I was humiliated. No other girl seemed to have the problems I had — or certainly never shared that they did. I was a failure as a female.

After a couple of years I learned to steal aspirin from our bathroom cabinet before the pains started, and hide my discomfort in public. The fainting stopped. I came close to passing out during the hours of SAT testing. But I didn't. I toughed it out.

When I was twenty-one I was diagnosed with endometriosis, and learned that my pains were not the same as those most women felt. That year I had the first of a series of eight surgeries to help control my condition. In those days the only hormonal treatment available was birth control pills, which helped a little, and my doctor trusted me with my first bottle of serious pain pills. I saw him every four to six months from then until he died, eight years ago.

But, despite his help, for most of my life from the time I was thirteen until I was in my late fifties, I was in pain, depending on those pills to get me through between surgeries. I was stubborn, and my doctor and I worked carefully together. I did not become addicted.

During those years I also traveled on company business, I was a supervisor, sometimes of large organizations, and I adopted and brought up four children on my own. Although I had to take time from the office for six weeks about every five years to have surgery, the only time I took individual sick days was when one of children was ill. Luckily, my crew was also healthy.

Most of my supervisors never knew of my medical condition. In a time when in most of my jobs I was the only management woman in my department, a "female illness" would have ended my career.

One vice president, signing off on a medical procedure my doctor and I had intentionally written up to be as unclear as possible, told me I'd be a lot more promotable if I'd just have a hysterectomy.

I was twenty-seven. He wasn't joking.

So — colds? Flu? Not me. I was tough. I was the one who took care of people. My children. The people who depended on me at work. My mother. Even my husband, who's had the misfortune to manage to have bad cases of the flu in several of the past years.

As he had this year over the Christmas holidays. And then managed to get again in late January.

And I'll admit, I gloated a bit. He didn't take vitamins. He didn't eat as many vegetables or fruits as I did. He didn't sleep as many hours a day. He needed to take better care of himself. And this time, the gods reached down and pointed at me.

Yes, I did all those things right. No, I almost never get colds. I don't think I've ever gotten the flu. And this was my very first time for … pneumonia. Yup. I got it good.

And I apologize to all the people (especially my husband) who put up with my actually thinking I was in control of my own body.

You all win.

Now I'm on antibiotics. There is hope I won't have to cancel any more talks and I'll actually get through the 976 emails in my in-box.

And I'll go back to eating my vegetables in their non-juiced form, and maybe even to sleeping in my own bed, and to doing some of the writing I was supposed to do in February.

But I'm newly chastened. I toughed it out for years. But — guess what? (Husband laughing in the corner.) Yes, I am human. I am not in control of everything. As my grandmother (who, years later, I realized had probably had endometriosis herself, before it was recognized as a disease) would have said – I got my comeuppance.

Forget the Corner Store:
Check the Police Blotter!

I suspect I've watched as many movies and TV shows set in small towns as the next person, and I can't help noticing that a lot of them get it wrong. Or at least out of date.

Almost all movies have at least one scene in which the local folks gather to exchange information (= gossip) at a small store, usually located in the center of town.

Now, when I was growing up, a few decades ago, there were such places in Maine. But supermarkets have invaded, and in most towns today the current equivalent of that old country store is a convenience store connected to a gas station. Not the same atmosphere at all.

There are still gathering places, of course. The post office in my town is a prime location. A lot of folks rent post office boxes just to have an excuse to stop in, and the place is buzzing in late morning, about the time the postmistress hangs the "Box Mail is UP!" sign.

She keeps track of what's happening, too. Once during a heavy snow storm I called her to ask if I'd received a thick envelope, since I was waiting for manuscript galleys, and their arrival would mean I'd have to go out in the storm.

Without checking, she immediately assured me that, "Yup. That envelope from Simon & Schuster came in this morning. And your husband got some pills you'd better pick up, and your granddaughter sent you a real nice postcard."

Good to know. I got myself up to the post office, just as she'd advised.

But the way to find out what's really happening is to read the weekly police reports in the local newspapers.

Some weeks the officers are too busy to provide any details and just list their accomplishments. ("The Boothbay Harbor Police Department conducted 22 motor vehicle stops, 2 welfare checks, attempted to locate one person, responded to 10 burglar alarms, 1 burglary, 13 medical emergencies, one harassment report, one juvenile problem, two unwanted subjects, one loud noise, 63 property checks, and assisted citizens six times.") This, of course, leaves the reader titillated and unfulfilled.

Did any of the burglar alarms have to do with the actual burglary? Did they find the person? What kind of unwanted subjects? How loud does a noise have to be to qualify for inclusion in a police report? And one juvenile problem? A young problem? Will it age? If there's only one young person in the entire area of Boothbay Harbor with a problem – that's a pretty quiet town. There was a time I had more than one just in my household.

Luckily, most weeks they give details. Of course, most

of their emergencies are not quite ready for prime time. "Officer Alfred Simmons investigated suspicious activity on Birch Point Road. Citizen claimed they heard someone open the screen door."

Clearly not a case for *Law and Order*. Since it's also the end of the listing, we can assume all was well. Not so when "Officer Kathy Williams investigated a complaint of criminal mischief on Old Dresden Road involving bullet holes in a mailbox." Yup. That's a problem. Better rent one of those boxes at the post office.

Then there are notices in which you hope perhaps words have been left out. "January 9. Josh Smith, 49, rolled backward into a school bus. No children on board were injured." I don't know Mr. Smith, but I also wondered about his health.

Usually names are given, but sometimes, for security or privacy reasons, not, as in "Officer Tyson Fait responded to a local business to remove a person who had been warned not to return there." Clear enough?

Officer Fait was in Damariscotta (I read a few newspapers in my area) where there were several people with inter-personal issues that week. The next listing was, "Officer Aaron Beck escorted a citizen to retrieve personal belongings, and assisted another citizen with questions regarding the safety of his children."

And, since it is Maine, there are sometimes local exigencies, as in this traffic report. "On December 17 Alice Cushman was operating a 2008 Chrysler PT Cruiser south on Route 96 when she went off the right side of the roadway and hit a utility pole. A snow squall passing through was a contributing factor." Kind of poetic.

In one week Wiscasset officers "responded to a car versus deer accident," "investigated suspicious activity near Wiscasset High School," "conducted a welfare check of subjects living in a van," (sad,) "dealt with unwanted subjects at a Gardiner Road residence," and "investigated the reported theft of two end tables from a front lawn." (No note on what end tables might have been doing on a front lawn in December in a snowstorm.)

But, by and large, as with all police departments, the majority of police tasks are motor vehicle stops, minor arrests, and calls for service. Embarrassing or helpful if they involve you or your neighbor, but not worthy of a major newspaper article.

In a recent copy of the *Lincoln County News*, however, the editor must have been smiling when he chose to place two 2-column articles side by side.

The first was headlined, "Round Pond Man Allegedly Assaults Girlfriend with ATV." Seems Adam Coffin and his girlfriend were staying in a tent at a friend's house. The girlfriend left the property "to take a walk," (sic) and Coffin ran her down with his ATV, knocking her into a ditch. She returned to the tent. He then followed her, kicked her, and swore at her. Later that night he went into the house and found her dancing with the homeowner. "The girlfriend attempted to escape through a bathroom window, but Coffin allegedly pushed her into the shower, where she hit her head, then choked her and threatened her. She contacted the police." At the time of the incident Coffin was out on bail for a previous domestic assault on the same woman. (He is now back in jail.)

That's a horrible story. Clearly the question is: why did the girlfriend stay around?

But now for the story in the very next column, headed, "Bristol Woman Jailed for Ramming Husband with Car." This case is much simpler. Seems Susan Aldrich and her husband were having an argument. She told him that if he came any closer to her she'd hit him with her car. He did. She did. His leg was broken. (Aldrich is now out on bail and forbidden use of alcohol.)

Makes me wish the girlfriend in the first story had had access to a car.

I can hardly wait to read the Sixth District Court Report to find out what happens next.

Collecting ... Stories and Scottish Jewelry

I've been involved with antiques all of my life.

My great-grandfather sold antiques and fine Scottish and Irish silver, crystal and linens in his Boston shop over a hundred years ago. My grandmother was a dealer in antique dolls and toys; her business was very like that of Gussie's in my *Shadows Antique Print Mystery Series*. And my mother and I were (and I still am, although I'm not as active as I used to be) antique print dealers.

I grew up in a family of both dealers and collectors. My father collected ivory carvings and scrimshaw. And then broken bank notes (paper money from American banks that went bankrupt.) My sister Nancy collected Thomas Nast cartoons and wood engravings and letters. My sister Doris collected miniature Mercedes-Benz cars, and vintage Fiesta ware dishes. Me? When I was a teenager I collected political memorabilia and old postcards and out-of-print Edith Wharton books. When I was older I collected special Christmas tree ornaments and old Santa Clauses.

My daughter Ali collects Niello jewelry from Thailand,

where she was born. My daughters Caroline and Elizabeth collect Spode Christmas Tree china. One of my grandsons has growing collections of baseball cars and LEGOs.

But in recent years tastes (and space) have changed. I've sold my political and postcard collections. My sister donated her Nasts to a museum. There is a limit to how much china you can actually use, and hundreds of Santas can become too many Santas.

Today I don't really collect anything (the thousands of books in my home don't count, really, because I use them as well as admire them. That's my story and I'm sticking to it.)

But I do have some family pieces I value, and that I won't part with.

One small collection I have is of Scottish jewelry. My grandmother always called it "Cairngorm" jewelry. She left a piece of hers to each of my sisters and to me.

In Scotland today it is called "pebble jewelry," and souvenir shops sell imitations of the real thing. In the Harry Potter movies, actress Maggie Smith wears one.

Real pieces are different colored agates and other Scottish stones set in sterling silver settings. They became popular, along with tartans, after Queen Victoria and Prince Albert bought their Scottish castle, Balmoral, in 1852. Victoria and Albert often dressed in tartans, and so did their children. Some of the first pieces of "pebble" jewelry were kilt pins.

Agates include amethyst, citrine, carnelian, jasper or bloodstone. They can be cloudy or clear or transparent.

Small pieces of stone are cut and set to be level with their silver settings. I have one piece which is just one stone; others have perhaps two dozen stones.

I first loved them because my grandmother loved them. And then I loved them more when I found out more about them.

For example, one of my pieces, in the shape of an anchor, has a special meaning. Anchor pins were worn by Scots who fished off the East Coast of Scotland, especially those sailing out of Aberdeen. Like the heavy sweaters they wore, knit especially for them by wives and mothers and sweethearts, the pins were worn to bring good luck on the waters and, if fate was not with their owner, to help identify his body so he could be brought home.

I love that my book *Seaward Born,* although not set in Scotland, pictured a drawing of an anchor very like my Scottish pin at the beginning of each chapter. That pin has inspired other stories, too. One of my "not ready for publication" books is about one of these anchor pins, and those who wore it.

I often look at the pieces of pebble jewelry I have and wonder about those who wore them before I did. Because, like all antiques, each piece has a story.

And that's what I've always thought collections were: symbols of the stories they told.

The Changing of the Seasons

This is the first April I remember that the trees on my road haven't been posted with bright orange signs warning that no heavy trucks are allowed to traverse these parts for a while.

If you lived here, you'd know why. In Maine, from the end of March until at least mid-May is usually mud season; the time when the winter snows and frosts melt, and people wear ankle-high "mud boots" (mine are bright yellow) if they're going to be walking on any unpaved surfaces. Even paved surfaces respond to mud season by sinking. Or at least cracking. Potholes multiply.

But this winter was so mild, and so dry, that right now we have green grass, and warmer than usual temperatures, and forest fire alerts. I've even seen some gardeners defy the adage that most vegetables should only be planted after Memorial Day.

This is a vacation week for most schools in Maine, so kids are taking full advantage of weather in the sixties and seventies. They're wearing shorts and begging to go to the beach. Monday was Patriot's Day — a state holiday we share with Massachusetts which commemorates the Battle of Lexington and Concord. It's one of the few remaining ties reminding us that until 1820 we were the District of Maine; the northern wilderness of Massachusetts.

Daffodils are in full bloom. Forsythia is out. Willow trees are in that special early stage of pale yellow green leaves. The cowbirds are back at our feeder, as are all the finches and the red winged blackbirds. The winter birds are learning to share again. Spring peepers are serenading us at night.

This unseasonal warmth is not all good. Maple sap came in so early, and the temperatures rose so high, that the harvest was half what it is usually. Maple syrup prices will be up this year. And we killed our first mosquito last week. Black flies probably won't be waiting for Mother's Day to appear, as they traditionally do.

The human population is increasing, too. Snow birds who live on Southport Island, near Boothbay Harbor, are arriving every day — the town water's been turned on. (Winter residents of the island have to have their own wells.) My neighbors across the street, who live in Boston, opened their house this weekend. We keep watching for our neighbors on the other side. They'll be driving up from Florida. They usually open their marina by May 1, so they should be here any day now.

Almost every day another seasonal restaurant opens, or at least puts out a sign announcing when the big day will be. Round Top Ice Cream opened, and we celebrated by having our first taste of raspberry truffle of the season. Gift shops will probably wait to open until Memorial Day.

When I was a child summer started on July 4, but today everything happens faster.

This morning I noticed some of the lobster traps that've been piled in a friend's yard all winter have migrated from the yard to his truck. I suspect within the next couple of weeks we'll be seeing his grass again, and he'll be out long hours in his boat.

My husband has been meeting with the other artists and craftspeople he shows with. They've been preparing new work all winter. Now they're planning their summer shows. They'll be up at the Stable Gallery in Damariscotta cleaning out the place in the next couple of weeks. Doors will open there May 12.

The Lincoln County Historical Association called. Would I train this summer's docents for the Old Lincoln County Jail in Wiscasset, where two of my historical novels are set? The Jail's summer hours start Memorial Day weekend.

Road crews are out, filling the potholes winter left behind, and cleaning winter sand off the roads. Other groups, some volunteers, some "volunteered", are cleaning up beaches, hiking trails, and the sides of highways. Spring cleaning in Maine is a state-wide chore.

Everyone's moving a little faster; smiling a little more. Schedules are a little tighter. Hopes are high. People will come to Maine, despite the gas prices. The economy's a little stronger. Home sales are a little better. That should be good for sales of art, high-end crafts, and antiques. Maine's restaurants have gotten some wonderful press.

The state's becoming even more popular as a destination.

Mainers love their state with a passion. But Maine's economy depends on sharing it with others. And so now, when Mother Nature is preparing for summer, Maine's residents are preparing for our summer guests. Some may call them the "summer complaints," but those folks from away, who head their cars and campers north-east, or who buy a ticket to Portland or Bangor, are also our summer residents, our relatives, our friends, and the people who make it possible for many of us to live in this place that we love.

We're tidying the place up. We're looking forward to having company. Every day a few more boats are in the harbors and a few more summer homes have flags flying. Farm stands are scrubbed and waiting for the first spring greens.

Maybe this is your year to head Down East. Looking forward to seeing you.

April Showers Bring ....
Mud Season

It isn't just April showers, despite that lovely little rhyme that Thomas Tusser came up with around 1557, that causes the mud. It's all the melting snow and ice that's still around, and the frozen soil defrosting, plus those April rains, which in my experience tend to be a lot heavier than showers. But Thomas Tusser lived in England, a few years back. Maybe they were showers then.

In any case, the result is the same. Mud. Lots of it.

Maine tries to get ahead of it by posting orange "Heavy Loads Limited" signs on many of the side roads (e.g. the roads most people live on) beginning in early March. If you read the small print, the sign instructs drivers that heavy trucks should stick to state roads until May 1, lest their weight result in even more pot holes, cracks, or breaks in the pavement. (Orange signs are posted on unpaved roads, too, for even more obvious reasons.)

In the meantime, mud is on cars. On shoes. On roads. On, in fact, pretty much anything outdoors, and on anything that HAS been outdoors.

April is also the time when to the outside eye Maine wakes up. Roads and bridges left to snow plows and local traffic all winter are suddenly decorated by orange cones and "under construction" signs.

Farmers' markets open, displaying their earliest (greenhouse grown) salad ingredients. The first wave of "See you in the spring!" restaurants and shops re-open, ready to greet the earliest snow-birds returning from Florida and the Carolinas in mid-April.

Near where I live, April 15 is the magic date everyone prepares for. No, not because it's tax day. Although we know that, too. April 15 is when town water is turned on for the large island of Southport. Summer folks have town water. If you live there year 'round, you have to have a well. So summer folks come back starting April 15, and businesses in nearly Boothbay Harbor, from the library to the hair salons and gourmet popcorn shop, gear up toward that date.

Farmers start looking at their fields. You can't plant in mud, but you can start preparing. Cold weather crops go in as soon as the ground dries a bit. Frosts can be expected until well into May, but that won't stop people from planting, and covering their seeds and young plants and crossing their fingers.

My husband plans to golf today. I'll suggest he wear his mud boots (ankle-high boots designed for times when sloshing and slurping are terms related to walking, not sipping beverages) but he probably won't. Men are stubborn. The Green won't be green — but it's April!

Time for golf!

Also time to dig out all the clods of earth the guy who plowed our driveway this past winter managed to dig out of one part of our lawn and deposit on another part. Somehow the crocuses have fought their way through this new layer of driveway stone and earth, but clean-up work needs to be done, along with picking up the truckload or two of branches that fell in our yard during winter storms, were covered by snow, dug into the mud, and now cover whole sections of what we hope is still lawn.

Time to put away the snakes (long stuffed pieces of sand or balsam-filled cloth that sit on all our window and door sills to keep out drafts during the winter), put on the mud boots and clean up the yard, turn out the outside water, put out the bird bath, and smile. Another few weeks, and the grass will be green.

Welcome, spring!

My First Date — and *Carousel*

I was a late bloomer, at least so far as dating was concerned. In high school I definitely fell into the "nerd" category. I only attended my senior prom in my role as editor of the high school newspaper. My "date" was the high school junior who was the newspaper photographer. I don't even remember whether we actually danced.

But during my summers in Maine no one knew I was a nerd.

The summer I was seventeen a young man from Boothbay Harbor (he was about twenty) invited me to go with him to a very special local event.

In 1955 the film adaptation of the Rogers and Hammerstein musical *Carousel* had been filmed in Boothbay Harbor. The stars, Gordon MacRae and Shirley Jones, had won the hearts of everyone in the region and signed autographs for many of them. Best of all, many residents of the Harbor had gotten jobs as extras in the film.

During the 1960s, before cable TV or videos or DVDs made it possible to see any movie at almost any time, the Opera House (aka movie theatre) in Boothbay Harbor would have one showing of *Carousel* each summer so everyone could come and once again relive the excitement of that filming, and see themselves on the big screen.

My date had been one of those extras. Not, you understand, anyone who could be identified in the film. He'd been one of the many young (and not so young) people hired to sail their boats across the harbor during the scene in which everyone is heading out to the island clambake.

Our evening involved joining practically the entire population of Boothbay Harbor (standing room only!) at the Opera House to see *Carousel*. You couldn't hear all the words in the movie, since everyone was busily pointing out themselves and their friends, singing along with the cast, talking about where parts of the film were shot, and remembering what Shirley Jones' favorite ice cream soda flavor had been at the local drugstore and who'd served her.

It was, I'll admit, a fun date. More fun than the relationship, which was short-lived. But I loved the movie. I still do.

Today few people remember *Carousel,* or remember it was shot in Boothbay Harbor. Even Carousel Wharf, where the song and dance "June is Bustin' Out All Over" was filmed, which for years was pointed out by tour boats, is now hard to locate. But it's still there, part of the Carousel Marina on Atlantic Avenue, a berth for visiting yachts on the east side of the harbor.

I read recently that plans are on the drawing board to

re-make *Carousel.*

If that ever happens, it would be wonderful if they'd consider coming back to Boothbay Harbor. Carousel Wharf is still there, and we still do great clambakes. That drugstore Shirley Jones visited is gone. But I'm sure we could find a way to get Round Top Ice Cream in Damariscotta to supply the cast and crew with ice cream sodas.

Maine is waiting. And in the important ways, it hasn't changed all that much since 1955.

Visiting My Characters …
in the Graveyard

Maybe I was born to be a mystery writer. One of my earliest memories is visiting the Mt. Auburn cemetery near Boston with my grandmother. I was just old enough to run a little ahead of her; not old enough to read. But I clearly remember the "angel" carvings on the oldest stones. She said they were angels. I thought they were scary faces.

As an adult I've wandered graveyards in several states, ranging from the Trinity Church Graveyard in lower Manhattan, which "in the day" was the place to buy and smoke pot on your lunch hour from the Stock Exchange, to the churchyard at St. Michael's Church in Charleston, South Carolina – the church that's on the cover of my *Seaward Born*. Signers of the Declaration are buried there, but my favorite stone's engraved with a man's name (which I've forgotten) and the words "He came to Charleston for his health and died." Succinct. And a little like an old stone in a graveyard near my home in Maine that lists no name. Just "Man from Vermont."

Since my graveyards of choice are eighteenth and

nineteenth century ones, in the past the only names I recognized were those of well-known people, like those signers of the Declaration. But now I write books set in the small seaport of Wiscasset, Maine, and many of my characters are real people who lived there. I feel I know them well, although we've never met. Sometimes I walk through the three old graveyards in town, stopping at the graves of those who people my books and apologizing to them for putting words in their mouths.

No, I don't really think they hear me in their current places of residence. But it reminds me that I'm writing about real people who walked the same streets I walk now.

Their graves tell parts of their stories. Jonathan Bowman, a respected lawyer who in my *Stopping to Home* marries eighteen-year-old Sally Clough, died two years later, at the age of 37. He's buried next to his first wife, Lydia. What happened to Sally? After his death she returned to her parents' home, and they moved to Thomaston after Jefferson's Embargo made it difficult for captains like her father to find work. Her mother opened a millinery shop in Thomaston, and Sally married the local minister and had fourteen children.

I suspect she didn't mind not being buried next to her first husband.

One small mystery to me is Dr. Theobold's gravesite. He was an army surgeon during the War of 1812, and then settled in Wiscasset and married Nancy, his first wife. She died in 1820 (an event in my book *Wintering Well*) leaving him with two young children. The doctor then remarried — twice — and survived those wives, too. It's clear in looking at his grave that he purchased the plot when Nancy died, and had matching stones engraved for both of them, with his own date of death to be added later. And so it was. But where were his second and third wives buried? I haven't been able to find out. Certainly not in his plot. His daughter Anne, who survived her father by many years, and her husband are buried in his plot. His son, also a doctor, but not in Wiscasset, is buried in another town.

My latest visit to a Wiscasset graveyard answered a question my research other places hadn't been able to answer. In *Uncertain Glory*, set in 1861, Edwin Smith, a wealthy young man in town, leads the town's recruits off toward their Civil War training camp. I knew he'd died a little over a year later, in the Battle of Fair Oaks, in Virginia. But the battle took two days. In the historical notes for my book I chose the second date — June 1, 1862 — as his date of death. But there, on the large monument his family erected, was the truth. He died May 31.

I found his grave just in time to correct the date in my book.

That historical detail might seem minor. But to him and his family, it was important. And so it was important to me. And, I hope, to my readers.

Being Married to an Artist

You probably know I'm a writer. You may not know that my husband, Bob Thomas, is an artist.

I was thinking the other night, as he and I were driving home from a gallery opening where his work was being shown, about what it was like to be married to an artist.

I've read blogs about what it's like to be married to a writer. We're distracted. We hear voices that aren't audible to others. (I won't say they aren't there, for obvious reasons.) We tend to leave scraps of paper around with strange notes on them. "Lily of the Valley poison? Strangled?" "Naked man on beach - sun burned or tan?" "Check width of 19th century chimneys."

Artists are different … in some ways. Since our home contains both (luckily for both our sanity, my study is on the second floor; Bob's studio is on the first,) I feel qualified to define some of the challenges (and advantages) to being married to an artist.

1. We don't have to worry about having too much wall space. Paintings hung in front of bookcases add another layer of insulation to help with long Maine winters.

2. My husband never has a problem choosing what to

wear. Everything he owns has dabs of paint on it. (The "good clothes" just have fewer dabs.) And, when he has to appear in public, he insists on wearing black. From underwear to outerwear. (I think he secretly believes that even white paint won't show on black.) At least it all matches.

3. Although he'll spend hours debating one line on a painting, the multicolored blobs of paint on the easel, floor, and table in his study are invisible to him, and even the dirt in his studio is sacrosanct. Somehow its displacement will disturb his muse. I just close my eyes and repress.

4. He can instantly analyze why an outfit I'm wearing does or doesn't work. I just have to watch that he doesn't recommend my black outfits all the time.

5. He likes to experiment. In all things. Usually in his studio, but, as I found when I opened the oven and found a painting baking there last week, not always limited to the studio. And ... not always limited to art. (Use your imagination on this one.)

6. As with many writers, the creative urge can strike artists at any time. It's not unusual for my husband to get up to paint at 2, 3 or 4 in the morning. Some artists demand natural light. My husband has a wood stove and "natural light" lamps. And we have electric bills. (And great paintings!)

7. Since my husband sees the world in colors and shapes, and I see them in words, we have constant discussions that go like this.

Him: "How do like the new painting?"

Me: "I like it. I like the faces in the trees beyond the river. Are they lions?"

Him: "What faces?"

Me: "Those tan circles. See - the eyes, and the mouth, and …"

Him: "They're not lions. They're nothing."

Me: "You should call it 'Lions in the Fog.'"

Him: "It's Altered Ground #137."

Me: "But that doesn't mean anything!"

Him: "It means whatever I want it to mean. Why don't you go have a cup of tea? I think I'm going to add some purple."

(I go make a cup of tea.)

8. Writers and artists create their books and paintings and then (since they both want to eat) try to sell their work. But writers can keep their words, even if they share them with the world. Artists have to say good-bye forever. There's a grieving process. An artist can't go back and look to see how he did something before; he can't admire or regret. If a painting is gone, it's gone. He can only begin again with an empty canvas or board. Selling a painting is a more emotional time than selling a book.

9. Both writers and artists get discouraged; feel they will never be able to create again; are sure everything they're doing is worthless; have dark times when the work is not going well at all. When an artist and a writer live together, they only hope the dark times don't come for both of them at once.

10. And when the good times come … when the paint is flowing, and the paintings are selling, and the world is admiring … then the fear is that it won't last. And that, too, is something another "creative" understands. So, frustrating though it is at times, being a writer married to an artist, means we appreciate the other's pain. We both admire and respect each other's space and work. And, best of all, we have each other to celebrate with when the world is going well.

It's a good life.

How My Editor
Changed My Family

I have a very limited personal history with pets.

When I was a toddler my mother had a pair of Siamese cats. But I was a sickly kid, and after one life-threatening asthma attack the doctor proclaimed I was allergic to cats. My mother's cats sadly disappeared, and we never had another one, fearing I'd either have health problems ... or, perhaps even worse, by the time I did have problems (I knew I wasn't immediately allergic to cats) my family would have become very attached to the cat.

Instead, my family, and then I, had parakeets. The first one was Happy. He talked ("Hello, pretty bird! Mommy is a pretty bird!") and often was allowed to fly around our large three-story home.

If we clapped, he'd come from wherever he was (Nibbling the wallpaper on top of one of the windows? Sitting in the crown of the ivory statue of Charlemagne who stood on a mantle in our living room? Picking up pieces of thread from my grandmother's sewing table?) One day my sister Nancy, used to Happy's riding on her head, walked out the back door with him perched there. Happy circled the back yard to check out freedom ... and then returned to Nancy's head when she clapped.

Happy was followed by Sunny, Enoch, Flit, Flirt, Flip, Flutter, Jinx, and others. When I was in college I even wrote a children's theatre play which included a parakeet, so I'd have an excuse to have one in my dorm room. He did an excellent job on stage.

After college I moved to Greenwich Village in New York City, where my roommate, Linda, and I bought a Weimaraner. His name was Justin, and he was clearly too large and needy for our apartment. We had him for about four months. Then Linda moved back to Connecticut for grad school and took him with her. He was the last pet I had any claim to owning.

My four daughters kept me busy enough.

But I write cozy mysteries. And for some reason, cats and cozies go together. In the *Shadows Antique Print Series* I gave my protagonist, Maggie Summer, a cat named Winslow Homer. Winslow wasn't a major character, but he was there.

Then, last January, on a Maine day with snow billowing outside my window, the editor for my new (*Mainely Needlepoint*) mystery series called. I immediately panicked. The manuscript for *Twisted Threads*, the first in that series, wasn't due until March 1. It wasn't finished. What if he wanted it early? I could be in big trouble.

But our conversation took an unexpected turn.

Editor: "I just called to see if there was a cat in *Twisted*

Threads."

Me: (thinking fast.) "No. Should there be a cat?"

Editor: (who is always right) "Cats are good."

Me: "Then there'll be a cat."

Editor: "What does the cat look like?"

Me: "Ah … how about a Maine coon cat?"

Editor: "Great!"

Me: (Getting a few more words in) "Why do you need to know about the cat now?"

Editor: "Because the art department is working on the cover of *Twisted Threads*."

I'll admit, I was impressed. They were working on the cover of a book no one (including the author) had read yet. But publishers do unexpected things. So I went back to my manuscript and gave Gram, the protagonist's grandmother and major series character, a cat named Juno. (She's the queen of the household.) And I finished the book.

But I'll admit — I had trouble writing Juno in at appropriate moments. Having never had a cat, I wasn't absolutely sure how she'd react to various scenes. Research was clearly needed. So I started looking more closely at all those cute cat videos people post on Facebook. (Or maybe I just liked cat videos.)

But that was secondary research. And whenever possible, research should be primary, right? So I found myself thinking about getting a cat.

I knew there might be a problem, should my allergies pop up again. But it turned out my husband liked cats almost as much as dogs. (We don't have one of those, either.) And he was willing to take the risk.

We decided that "sometime" we'd adopt a cat.

Cynthia Lord, one of my author friends, volunteers at the Coastal Humane Society, not far from us. (Among other books, she writes a wonderful series for young readers called the *Shelter Pet Squad* series. Write what you know!)

So when Cindy posted that the Humane Society was having a special adoption night June 1, my husband and I were intrigued. Maybe this was our time. Maybe we'd adopt an older cat, we thought.

We headed for Brunswick, wondering how many people would show up for an event that started at midnight. To our amazement, when we got to the building an hour before midnight (when they would start placing the animals) we found a full parking lot. People of all ages were there to meet the cats at midnight.

Asked, "Are you here to adopt?" we said "Yes," even though we hadn't officially decided this was our time. We were assigned number twenty three.

Then we waited, with dozens of other people, of all ages. There were balloons. Popcorn. Coffee. Movies for the kids. But the big event, meeting the cats and kittens who could be adopted, wouldn't start until the clock struck twelve.

When that happened, people who had the first ten numbers were allowed in to see the cats, whose cages had been uncovered. Caught up in the excitement at midnight, we stood in line and peeked over the wall separating the cages area from the people waiting.

Maybe if there were two older cats who were friends, we could take two? Bob shared that he'd always liked black cats. I didn't have a preference.

But, hmm. A mystery writer with a black cat. That might work.

We saw two cages of awfully cute orange and white kittens.

But Bob was still talking about black cats, and I'd heard (on Facebook, my source for all things cat) that black cats were always the last to be adopted. And I'm a sucker for someone (or some animal) who really needs a home.

We'd thought of adopting an older cat. But the kittens were so cute!

Finally it was our turn. Bob checked out all the black cats. ("Com'on guy. Come to the front of the cage so people will see you! You won't get adopted hiding in the back!")

Two older cats were in one cage, to be adopted together. By us? We couldn't decide. (They weren't black.) So many possibilities. One year-old cat needed to go to a home without any other animals. That wouldn't be a problem for us.

Then we looked at the kittens. Black and white. Orange and White. Tiger. Some already wore the yellow collars that meant they'd been chosen. We kept looking, confused by all the variations. But it was clear adopting a kitten had become a possibility.

Then, in the far corner, we found four more cages of kittens that other people were, at that moment, ignoring. One cage held two black kittens, active and fluffy. One already wore a yellow collar. We took the other one out. She jumped to Bob's shoulder.

"This one's ours," he pronounced. I agreed. Soon she had a yellow collar with our name on it. She was two months plus two days old and weighed 1.9 pounds. She'd been spayed the week before. She'd originally come from another shelter.

When we lined up to have our picture taken with our new family member (already named "Shadow,") we were number fifty in adoptions that night. (Some people had adopted two or more cats.) Shadows was so small she barely showed in the photograph.

By 3:30 in the morning Shadow was home, equipped with a litter pan and water and food in our bedroom so she wouldn't feel overwhelmed by the whole house. She didn't sleep much that night. Neither did we.

In the months since Shadow has decided that my study is her playroom. She takes pencils out of my pencil holder, chases them across my desk, and pushes them onto the floor. She likes to sit in the window and watch the bird feeder below. When we sleep, she sleeps. She is a Velcro-cat. Where we are, she is. Right now I'm typing with her on my lap. This is the second time I've written this essay. She deleted the first draft. Guess it wasn't up to her standards.

So we now have an eight-month old black cat. Yes, Juno is also in the books following *Twisted Threads*. And my main character, Angie Curtis, may even get a cat of her own in a book or two.

I've learned about cats. I've learned they rip notes off your bulletin boards. Tear wallpaper off the wall. Feel entitled to sleep on (or in) your bed with you. Shadow has changed our lives in ways we couldn't have imagined.

And for now, allergy-free (knocking on wood,) thanks to an editor in New York, thousands of readers who love cats in mysteries, and a friend who volunteers at the Humane Society, for the first time in my life I own a cat.

Although, according to what I've seen on Facebook, maybe that cat now owns me.

Gardening and Dreams

When I think of my grandparents, especially my grandmother, I think of her gardens. In her home in Roslindale, Massachusetts, where I spent some of my earliest years, she had a wonderful large rectangular rose garden, with an oval brick path in the middle that I loved to run around. I also loved to fill jars with the Japanese beetles that ravaged those roses - and pull off their legs.

So her garden wasn't entirely a romantic experience. At least for the Japanese beetles.

After my grandfather retired, my grandparents shared a home with my parents in New Jersey in the winter months, and, in the summer, shared the home in Maine where I live now.

My grandparents would head for Maine as soon as they deemed it warm enough — usually in early April — so they could start gardening. They installed a kidney-shaped iris garden near the porch, and a large garden near the barn which included raspberry bushes, vegetables, and flowers. The raspberries were especially important to them since during the hard days of the Depression when they'd lived in New York City they'd dreamed of being able to grow and eat raspberries.

My grandmother would get up early to "beat the birds to the berries," and lay the damp, ripe red raspberries she'd picked to dry on card tables set up for the occasion at one end of our large kitchen. Later in the day the berries would be turned into raspberry pies or shortcakes — or, if not perfect, jams, jellies, or syrups for the winter months.

But raspberries weren't all she grew. Tomatoes were canned. Mint became mint jelly for winter lamb. And, of course, we had fresh flowers all summer, and fresh salads, and vegetables for the table. I helped to some extent by weeding and picking berries and vegetables and stirring sauces and straining jellies, but my mother and grandmother did most of the work. By the time I was old enough to make a major contribution I was assigned to lawn mowing, and by fourteen I had a summer job as well. But the garden, and its products, were all part of our summers in Maine.

When I had my first home in New Jersey I, too, had a garden. I planted daffodil bulbs in the fall because I loved spring flowers, and I grew vegetables and a few annuals in the summer. I was a single parent, and the vegetables helped with my budget as well as being fun to grow. The snow peas seldom made it to my stir fries: my daughters ate them off the vines. I loved that.

Somehow, despite working full-time and studying for my doctoral comps, I remember canning tomatoes until the wee hours of the night (or morning,) and being proud of the line of canned tomatoes and tomato sauce on the shelves lining the steps to our basement.

One year dozens of tomatoes ripened just as we were to leave for our Maine vacation. Not wanting to lose that fruit, I packed two grocery bags full of ripe or near-ripe tomatoes, put them on the passenger seat next to me, the children in the back seat, and headed north. I figured I'd make tomato sauce in Maine.

It was a hot July day. As we drove through New Jersey and New York traffic, the tomatoes kept ripening. And, as I took a sharp right exit turn onto the Merritt Parkway in Connecticut ... both bags of tomatoes fell. Sideways. Onto me.

To shrieks of delight from my daughters, I drove the remaining six hours to Maine covered with smashed, ripe tomatoes. In our family, that turn will forever be known as "the tomato turn."

It turned out that was my last garden. I moved again, to a larger house, when my family grew, but although I started a garden there, no plants thrived. We were on a hill, and there was little topsoil.

The lawn was mostly moss, and even my daffodils refused to naturalize, although every fall I persistently planted more bulbs.

So when I finally was able to move to Maine full-time, one thing I wanted to do was bring back the gardens. They had long since disappeared; there'd been no one to take care of them since my grandparents died so, gradually, they'd been taken over by lawn. I hired someone with a tractor and started again. I planted vegetables and flowers.

That first year I was busy, writing, and taking care of my mother, and didn't give the garden the care it needed. The flowers survived to some extent. The vegetables provided fodder for various types of insects and the local woodchuck. But I discovered, to my delight, that the violets and Johnny jump-ups that my grandmother had loved appeared, as though by magic, in the places she had planted them, so many years before.

In the fall I planted daffodils.

And they bloomed in the spring.

I soon realized my writing and my family were more important to me than my garden, so it, too, is now gone; all that's left is the slate path I laid that first year. And the daffodils I planted all over our lawn delight me every spring. I add to them regularly.

And every May, near that slate path in the grass, the violets come back, reminding me that my grandmother lived her dream here, in this house; in this yard. She wanted a garden, with raspberries. And she made that happen.

I, too, had a dream. I wanted to write. And I'm making that happen. Her violets are here as witnesses. I don't think she'd be disappointed that I haven't continued her garden. I think she'd like that this house is still a place where dreams come true.

Why Antiques?

Recently I attended a symposium on Maine antiques run by the Maine Antique Dealers Association, of which I'm a former board member, and The Kennebunkport Historical Society. Most people who attended the symposium were antiques dealers, auctioneers and museum directors.

A major theme of the symposium was "How do we get young people to be interested in and value antiques?"

It got me thinking about what fascinates me about antiques, and when that interest started.

I'm a fourth generation antiques dealer. My great-grandfather, who I knew only when he was in his late nineties, imported Irish and Scots linens, crystal, and furniture for his shop on Beacon Hill in Boston from about 1890-1910. His oldest daughter, my grandmother, was a doll and toy dealer in the 1940s and 1950s. Some of my earliest memories are of going with her to antique shops and shows and auctions. One of her dealer friends, Mrs. Jacques in Marblehead, Massachusetts, gave me the first book in my collection when I was about six: a first edition of Kate Douglas Wiggin's *Rebecca of Sunnybrook Farm*. She made sure I knew it was a treasure. I still have it.

I remember my grandmother advising me to spend my allowance on paper dolls of film stars and television characters, and not to cut them out. To save them, because they'd be valuable in the future. She was right.

Hitchcock, Waterford, Parian, Limoges, French Fashion Dolls, Schoenhut circuses and pianos, black-headed china dolls, McLaughlin, peddler dolls, were all part of my vocabulary by the time I was in second or third grade. My grandmother would point at a tea caddy or a silver box or a painting in her home, and tell me who it had belonged to in the past, and why it was treasured. I knew that if you tired of an antique you could resell it and buy something even more special; if you spent your money at a candy store it was gone forever. I knew antiques were usually made more carefully than their modern equivalents. That they were often beautiful. That they were links to people and places in the past.

I began to collect a few things. Politics fascinated me, so I collected political memorabilia … campaign buttons, tokens, tickets to political conventions, and related items. Postcards were inexpensive, so I collected some of those, too, learning that "Detroits" were more valuable that other American publishers. I especially valued postcards promoting women's right to vote.

Researching and collecting was part of who I was. It was built into budgets and vacation plans from the time I was a young teenager. I knew antiques were not only a hobby, but an investment.

I always thought that one day I, too, would become an antique dealer, and when I was in my twenties it seemed a logical step. I couldn't afford to leave my corporate job, but I started small. My mother, who had recently retired, volunteered to run my business, so I provided the first funding, did the accounting, and we shared the buying.

In those first years my mother did most of the selling. At first we were generalists, featuring kitchen wares and country "smalls," as they're known in the business. But soon my mother, an artist, became fascinated by antique prints, and I, too, got involved. We became antique print dealers. We talked of opening a shop, but my mother lived in Maine and I lived in New Jersey, and neither of us wanted to be tied to shop hours. We did antique shows in the northeast, and saw customers by appointment.

As my mother got older and found shows more difficult to do, I got more involved, until we always did shows together or occasionally I did a show by myself. My daughters helped me carry inventory and set up. Some were more interested in the business than others, but all had their favorite prints, and even my first granddaughter became familiar with antique shows.

My mother did her last antique show with me only three months before she died, at the age of 89. After she died, I continued the business with my husband as my partner.

I still have a large inventory of prints, but the antiques business was hit hard by the 2008 crash. For the first time in the thirty five years I'd been in business I found myself losing money at antique shows. And at the same time I was spending more time writing. So after a couple of years my husband and I decided to just do one or two shows a year, and see customers by appointment or by mail.

Sitting with a room full of lovers of antiques yesterday, I felt again the friendship and camaraderie of those who also valued the glimpses of the past that antiques give us all. The deeper understanding of how our ancestors lived, which now helps me write my historical novels. The joy of discovering a piece that is unique. Special. History that touches one's heart.

Today not many young people see the value and the heritage of antiques. It's a problem for the antiques business, but I think it's also a problem for our shared view of our place in history. Newer is not always better. Crafts and passions of the past can enrich lives today.

Many young people — and I'm referring to people up through their thirties and perhaps older – seem intimidated by the antiques I found so fascinating and accessible when I was young. They don't attend antiques shows and auctions. They don't care about the past, or its accoutrements.

To me, that's sad. Because antiques are traces, "shadows," as I write in my mystery series about an antique print dealer, of the past. Windows into where we came from.

And if the past, and the lessons it has to share with us, are ignored, we as a society will lose a special perspective on how we got to where we are now.

Boothbay Harbor's Fishermen's Festival

Lots of festivals are held in Maine. The Lobster Festival in Rockland. The Clam Festival in Yarmouth. The Franco-American Festival in Waterville. The Highland Games in Topsham. The Balloon Festival in Great Falls. The Moxie Festival in Lisbon. Windjammer Days. County Fairs. An assortment of strawberry festivals and blueberry festivals.

There used to be a Blueberries and Moose Festival, but it, sadly, was discontinued. All of those festivals are scheduled during summer months, and are designed to provide fun, photo opportunities, plenty of local food, entertainment for visitors to Maine — and employment and income for residents. (Those of us who live here have also been known to enjoy a clam roll and a bottle of Shipyard Ale at one or more of those festivals, too.)

But a few festivals are reserved for Mainers themselves. One of those is the annual Fishermen's Festival in Boothbay Harbor, the thirty-ninth of which was held this April. The Fishermen's Festival celebrates working fishermen and their heritage. There's no glitz, no glamour, and no souvenirs, although you could buy a cup of coffee or a tee-shirt from seniors at Boothbay Region High School raising money for their graduation party. Most people attending live in Boothbay Harbor or one of the surrounding towns.

The festival started Friday night with a haddock dinner, followed by the Shrimp Princess Pageant, in which a dozen young ladies between the ages of nine and twelve demonstrated their talents (most sang, but one played the violin and one jumped rope), and the winner was chosen Shrimp Princess. After the pageant those so inclined could adjourn to a local restaurant where *Jehovah and the Holy Mackerels* were playing until 1 a.m.

Saturday there was food, beginning at 6 a.m. with a pancake breakfast at the Lions Club, and moving on to a fish fry and a lobster bake that basically went on all day, and ending with a church supper at the Congregational Church (two seatings, one at 5 and one at 6 p.m.).

Saturday was cold, even for a Maine April. Temperatures were in the high twenties, with 20-30 mph winds gusting from the ocean, when my husband and I arrived at 8 a.m., in time to see the Codfish Races.

The Codfish Races (relay races in which young people hand off large slippery fish to the next in line to run) were followed by the Bait Shoveling Race, the Trap Hauling Competition, and, one of the highlights of the day, the Lobster Crate Running — in which participants must run along the tops of lobster crates strung between two town docks. A fall means a dunking in forty degree water. There was also Dory Bailing, Oyster Shucking, and an assortment of less strenuous activities for the youngest kids.

But if Saturday was the fun day, Sunday was really the heart of the festival.

Early Sunday afternoon the people of Boothbay Harbor gathered, as they do every year, at the Fishermen's Memorial on the east side of the harbor to honor area fisherman lost at sea. This is not done casually. The names of the 229 men whose names are engraved on the Memorial are read out loud, and a bell tolls for each of them.

The first name is that of Captain John Murray, 27, who died May 17, 1798. Many of the names are from the same families: fathers, sons, brothers, fishing together. The worst single disaster was in October of 1851, when the *S.G. Matthews* was lost, taking with it thirteen men, eight of them under the age of twenty-one. Fishermen begin their profession young. Martin Lewis was only eleven when he was lost at sea in 1845.

Many attending this year's service were holding a list of the names read; each year it's printed in the local newspaper. Many of them were related to men whose names were listed. (No women are on the list. Yet.) The names read are Boothbay names. Preble. Clark. Tibbetts. Greenleaf. Gardener. Reed. Hodgdon. Townsend. Pinkham.

The last name carved on the monument is that of Roy Bickford, who died October 13, 2003. He fell overboard while lobstering aboard the *Sharon Marie* near Pemaquid.

By next April's Fishermen's Festival there will be another name on the memorial. The men and women listening to the reading of the names this year were all too aware that just one week before the festival the body of lobsterman Earl Brewer was found, adrift, south of Squirrel Island. He had been alone on his fishing boat, the *Sea Foam*.

After the reading of the names fishing boats circle the inner harbor and pass the Fishermen's Memorial so the fleet can receive blessings from the local clergy for a safe and profitable year.

Maine may seem a scenic and somewhat romantic, perhaps even old-fashioned, vacationland, to many. But for those who make their living from the waters, lobstering and fishing are still, over two hundred years since Captain John Murray lost his life at sea, hard and risky ways to make a living.

For the fishermen of Boothbay Harbor and their families, taking time once a year to relax, celebrate their heritage, and acknowledge the risks of the new season, are reasons enough for a festival.

The Ells of Maine

My house has an ell.

If you're from, or know, Maine or northern New England, that will come as no surprise to you. But several times I've mentioned ells in my books set in Maine (I even set a fire in one in *Shadows on the Coast of Maine,*) and I've gotten letters asking, often with a bit of embarrassment, "Just what is an 'ell?'"

Since I grew up with them, I was surprised when a little research showed me that ells are only common in Maine, a few other parts of northern New England, Connecticut, and a few towns in northern New York State, where folks from Maine moved during the nineteenth century.

Although some characteristics of the New England ell are found in other parts of the country (some attached southern "summer kitchens" are similar) there is something special about this type of Maine architecture that never caught on anywhere else.

In 1984 Thomas C. Hubka wrote a book about it. He called the book, *Big House, Little House, Back House, Barn: The Connected Farm Buildings of New England.* Since then, many people have referred to a home of this kind as a "Big House/Little House/Back House/Barn" type. But old timers still call it simply, "A house with an ell."

So — what exactly is an ell? It's the series of connecting rooms (Hubka called them buildings) between the main house and the barn. Originally, as in my house, the first room, the one closest to the main house, included a back stairway to the second floor of the ell, which included a bedroom for a hired man or two, and an attic for storing dried food for winter. The first floor would be a "modern" kitchen — usually one with a wood stove, not a fireplace (fireplaces were in the main house,) and perhaps a sink with a pump, and a place near the wood stove chimney to heat water for washing.

The main house contained the parlor(s) and the formal dining room and front door, and looked out at the road. Whenever geography permitted, it faced either east or west. The back of the house faced north, and would be hit by winter winds, so it had the fewest windows and doors.

The door to the kitchen in the ell faced the dooryard, a working area where there might be an herb or small vegetable garden, a well, an area for drying clothes, a place for chopping wood and a large woodpile for winter.

Generally the dooryard was cluttered with projects too big or messy to be performed indoors, from butchering to repairing tools or vehicles. The dooryard of a farm would, of course, contain very different activities than the dooryard of a sea captain's home. Children played in dooryards, close to the house, where the barn at one end of the ell and the main house at the other end protected them from winds.

What about the other rooms, or buildings, in the ell? That would depend on the household. If the family kept cows or goats, there might be a room for making and storing butter or cheese. There might be an icehouse. A room for quilting or spinning or dying. Farthest from the house, or even in a corner of the barn (which was reached through a door in the farthest room) was the privy. Somewhere there was space for storage of dry wood, moved from the outside to dry before being moved to fireplaces or stoves. Storage of fine tools.

No two ells were the same; no two families' needs were the same.

But when bitter winter winds blew, and snows piled high, Mainers who had ells between their barns and their houses could reach their animals and their privies without going outside. It was an efficient and economical system.

Homes were built this way beginning about 1800, although the style was most popular from about 1840 until 1890.

The home I live in, for example, was originally built in 1774 on an island. I know from records left that it had a barn at that time, but probably did not have a connecting ell. When it was moved to the mainland in 1833, however, it was updated: an ell and attached barn were added, and a new kitchen in the ell replaced the old-fashioned fireplace kitchen in the original house.

The house is set in the classic way: the back was to the

north, the dooryard to the warm south, the front door to the west, and barn to the east.

And the ell? Yes, it's a little like the letter "L". But it's so much more.

Twelve Simple June Pleasures

Even though I spend a lot of time writing, or thinking about writing, other parts of life are important, too. The changing seasons, for example. In Maine, June marks the official change to summer. It's a month when I especially savor

1. Reading on the porch overlooking the river with a glass of wine or frosty lemonade with fresh-picked mint.

2. Watching the sun set over the river.

3. Seeing lupine blooming in fields and along roadsides.

4. Cheering on the goldfinches, chickadees and cardinals busily searching for food for their families and waiting to see them introduce their chicks to our bird feeders.

5. Keeping the windows wide open at night, but sleeping under a blanket.

6. Grilling dinner. (Technically – watching my husband grill dinner.)

7. Smelling freshly mown grass and mud flats and salt water.

8. Seeing rainbows after thunder storms.

9. Luxuriating in long, long days of sunlight.

10. Waving at neighbors seldom seen during winter months who in June stop in for a word or libation on their way to their home or boat.

11. Hearing children playing, lobster boats on the river, tractors mowing lawns, baby birds squabbling at the feeder, and train whistles echoing across the river. Someone used to play his bagpipes in the late afternoon on an island nearby. No one plays now. I miss hearing the bagpipes.

12. Tasting fresh greens and vegetables and cheeses from the farmer's market. And knowing that we'll have three more months to enjoy warm weather.

Thoughts While Whale Watching

There are both advantages and disadvantages to living in a vacation area.

I've learned to keep clean sheets on the guest beds, hamburger in the freezer, and pots in which to make chowder, cook pasta, and boil lobsters at the ready. My husband knows every farmers' market within twenty miles. I try not to have book deadlines between June and September.

But the past month has offered special challenges.

It has rained. Almost every day. Any moment now (yes; it's raining) we may break the 139 year record for "wettest recorded summer in Maine history." I've had guests who stayed two weeks and never saw the sun.

Now, there are alternatives to outdoor Maine. One of my guest rooms is also my "mystery and suspense room" — two walls of floor-to-ceiling bookcases filled with mysteries. I have VHS and DVD movies. Maine boasts art galleries, craft shops, museums, outlet stores, and innumerable places to buy souvenirs and lobster rolls.

I encourage folks "from away" to partake of all of Maine's largesse, not just its (now sodden) beaches, (foggy) cliffs, and (muddy) trails.

Luckily, many of my guests are readers, and curling up with one of the many books in our home, or making a stop at a nearby independent book store for the latest of whatever the particular guest's literary taste calls for is not a bad way to spend a vacation, especially if you add a glass of wine (or sparkling cider, for younger guests) and the prospect of a lobster salad or some of my husband's garlic-steamed mussels.

By and large, all have coped well.

But one day two weeks ago – perhaps by magic – the sun appeared. A decision was made quickly. Whale watching! A telephone call. An hour later we were off to sea.

The afternoon was perfect. Just warm enough. Blue sky. And – whales? Two pods; some within yards of the boat. It *was* magical.

I turned from searching the horizon for yet another whale. A woman was sitting on the deck, leaning against the boat's cabin, totally oblivious to those excitedly pointing out whales and seals and glorying in the perfect day.

She was reading.

I'm an author. I had to know what the book it was. So I peeked. It was a fantasy, *Graceling*. I'd read it. And, yes, there is magic there.

I didn't speak to the woman. But what I wanted to say was, "Sometimes reality is magical, too. The story will be there when this hour is over. The whales, and the scent of the sea, will not. Put down the book, and don't forget to live your own life."

But I didn't. Because there have been times when I, too, have needed the comfort of a book more than I wanted views of wild waves and the horizon.

And I suspect that's true of many readers.

Tastes of a Maine Summer

It's (finally) summer in Maine. Not that the other seasons aren't special here along the coast … but summer is different.

It's the only time of the year out-of-state license plates outnumber those proclaiming "Vacationland."

It's the time when the motel up the road from me is a little embarrassed its permanent sign reads "Now! Heated Units!"

It's the month when back-to-schoolers swarm through the outlets in Freeport and the Staples in Brunswick.

And it's the busiest time of the year for farmers' markets. Home-made cheeses, eggrolls and cinnamon rolls are as available there as blueberries, zucchini, tomatoes and "free range eggs." This year my husband is usually the one patronizing the local markets since I'm trying to make a September 1 manuscript deadline (*Threads of Evidence*) and prepare for a September 6 publication date (*Shadows on a Maine Christmas*). He brings the market home to me.

This is the time of year for some of my favorites: fried summer squash. Mussels in herbed wine. Scalloped tomatoes. Blueberry pie, cake, pancakes, and muffins. Just-picked sweet corn. (Simmering the cobs and leaves results in a fantastic broth that will be the basis for corn chowder later on.) Lobster, of course. My current favorite way to eat it is in a lobster club sandwich with crisp bacon and fresh tomatoes and lettuce. Yum! (Lobster broth is also simmered and used later for haddock chowder.)

My husband, who grew up in Beirut, Lebanon, makes hummus. We nibble it, along with locally made cheeses, on our porch overlooking the river. He indulges in wine or Scotch. I'm limited to lemonade for a while. With deadlines approaching, I'll go back to writing or editing after dinner. Dinner itself? Perhaps panko-fried haddock. Sliced tomatoes. Cole slaw made from young cabbage and carrots. That sweet corn. For dessert? Locally made ice cream with berries to top it if we feel in the mood to indulge.

Or perhaps just steamed mussels with French bread to dunk in the wine and herb and butter broth. I'd be embarrassed to tell you how many mussels we can consume at one meal. Like the local oysters and clams available this time of year, they taste of the sea.

They taste of summer.

Choruses of Inspiration: Chipmunks in the Fall

I have a special fondness for those small busy little creatures who spend spring through early fall zooming back and forth between their elaborate passageways under my front yard to the place they love best, where food rains down from dawn until dusk: under my bird feeders.

They comfortably share this space with mourning doves, the occasional crow, and other birds too large or too clumsy to cope with the feeders above, or who are just waiting their turns there.

But while the birds come and go, the chipmunks are seldom gone for longer than it takes them to duck through the barn or under our porch to return to their storehouse, deposit their latest cache of sunflower seeds, and return.

This time of year their gathering, and their kibitzing with other chipmunks, increases. If you've ever shared space with chipmunks, you'll recognize their calls. I don't speak chipmunk, but their loud "chipchipchip" is hard to miss. I've heard it repeated for as long as fifteen minutes, and then be answered by others as far as an acre away.

There's also a softer call, which doesn't last as long.

The generations of chipmunks who've inhabited the land around our house (and occasionally made forays into the house itself) have also occasioned stories.

The summer before my senior year in college I was writing plays for children's theatre as part of my senior thesis. Curious about how close the chipmunks would come to me while I was working, one day I put my typewriter on the porch floor and sprinkled sunflower seeds on the keys.

The chipmunks came, sitting on the keys and investigating this new feeding station.

The result was a series of pictures, one of which I put at the front of my thesis. I dedicated my work to "That Elusive Spirit."

Surely chipmunks, who worked so hard, stayed alert to their environment, and called to their friends to warn them of dangers and keep in touch with their progress (or so I imagined) while saving for the cold days ahead, were role models.

I now have a small porcelain chipmunk in my study, looking at me seriously, reminding me that work must be finished before play.

When Tori, my oldest granddaughter, who has Down Syndrome, was about seven, she was happily watching TV on the floor of our living room while I'd backed my van up to the open kitchen door and was packing for an antique show.

Suddenly she called me. "Nonnie! Come!" When I

reached the living room she looked up at me indignantly. "Nonnie! Chipmunk in our house! Tell him to go home. This is our house. Not his." She then turned back to the TV.

I glanced around the living room. Sure enough. A very confused chipmunk was perched on the back of one of our armchairs. (Chipmunks are curious, and the open back door was near the bird feeders.)

My granddaughter watched approvingly as I opened the living room door to the porch and shooed the chipmunk around the room until he zoomed out, back to "his place." Order had been restored. (Although I have on other occasions found mysterious caches of sunflower seeds under cushions in that same room.)

My husband, a relative newcomer to Maine, quickly fell under the spell of the chipmunks. His favorite chipmunk activity is what he calls, "chipmunk races." Two chipmunks run up the ramp to our porch, and then race like mad for the length of the porch, under chairs, tables, around anyone who happens to be there at the time, and then jump off the end of the porch — over four feet, to the ground. Why? We have no idea.

Chipmunks don't hibernate, but they are "dormant" in the wintertime. (My husband says they're like men: they sleep for a while, and then get up, eat a little, go to the bathroom, and then go back to sleep.) Only rarely do they leave their burrows. Sometime in October, depending on the temperature, the chipmunks will quietly (or not so quietly!) close up shop, find a cozy corner in one of the many rooms they've made off the passages in their network of storage rooms, and fall asleep. A well-deserved rest. And we won't be entertained or inspired by their work ethic or antics until early next spring.

They'll be missed. The return of the chipmunks is one of our most treasured measures of spring.

First Years … First Memories

I've been working on the third book in my Mainely Needlepoint series, *Thread and Gone*. If you haven't read the first one, *Twisted Threads*, Angie Curtis, the main character, is from Haven Harbor, Maine. Her mother disappeared when she was ten years old. Angie left Maine when she was eighteen, but now she's back, to find her mother's killer and start a new life.

As Angie visits places she hasn't seen since her childhood, and meets people she knew as a girl, her memories haunt her. Good memories and not-so-good memories. When I'm writing from her point of view, memories are on my mind.

So when I saw an article in *This Week* magazine called "Why We Forget Our First Years" I read it.

The article said that most adults do not remember their first three or four years, and have very few memories of what happened before they were about seven. Would returning to a home where they'd lived as a child or meeting a long-lost relative bring those memories back? Not according to this author. He wrote that until the 1980s, that was what was believed. But a 1987 study showed that many two and a half year old children could describe events that had taken place six months before. Children between the ages of four and ten could recall incidents that happened when they were only two years old. But interviewed again two years later, two-thirds of these same children had forgotten those incidents.

Called "childhood amnesia," the study showed that most of our childhood is forgotten. Gone. The memories we do keep are sometimes connected to emotions, and sometimes totally random.

Does what happened in those early years matter, if we can't remember them? Psychologists say yes; even if we can't remember the details of our early life, those events imprint on our emotions, so in later years we believe circuses are fun (or scary ;) dogs are good; cats scratch. Grownups can be trusted. Or not.

I have three memories from before I was two and a half. I remember being outdoors, bending down to look through a cellar window, and seeing a bunny inside.

I remember climbing a lot of stairs and finding a room at the top of the stairs on the right that was filled with cartons and my doll's swing, on top of the boxes, in a spot of sunlight by the far window. I remember holding my grandmother's hand and walking through a tunnel of white snow, away from my house.

When my mother was still alive I shared those memories with her, and she agreed they were real. The bunny lived in the basement of the house next door to where we lived until I was two. The room I remembered (and which became my own room years later) was on the third floor of the house we moved into a month before my little sister was born. And that's when my grandmother came to New Jersey and took me back to Boston with her so my mother could unpack and rest before her next baby was born.

My grandmother and I left New Jersey right after a heavy snowfall and took the train to New York, and then to Boston. I have no recollection of that train ride.

I have many memories of my grandparents' home, and of people and things there. They left that house to move in with us when I was nine, so the memories must be of events before then, but I can't date them.

When I'm writing Angie Curtis' memories I'm assuming she can remember repeated events, like Fourth of July fireworks and Christmas. And she can remember emotional events, like special days she spent with her mother.

But, of course, I'm writing fiction.

How far back do our memories go? And how often do we think of them? I'm not a psychologist, but I suspect those are important questions. And, as a writer, even if I can't answer the questions for myself, I can answer them for my characters.

Living in Maine versus
Vacationing Here

Although many people (from away) now consider me a Maine writer, I am very conscious of the fact that a) I was born in Boston. And b) I've only lived in Maine full-time since 1998.

Of course, I vacationed here ("vacationed" being defined as anywhere from ten days to ten weeks while I was in school and/or working) for (gulp) over fifty years before that. In only one year did I fail to get to Maine: the first year after I'd graduated from college and had a "real" job. The kind of corporate job where you didn't get any days off for the first twelve months. My mother sent me a framed sprig of sea lavender with a note "not to forget." That framed sprig was on my office desk every one of the thirty years I worked in New York and New Jersey. I didn't forget. And I wished for Maine breezes.

Now, miraculously, I'm here. Dream come true. I work for myself — although frequent emails from one of the four companies that have published my books remind me that I still have deadlines. But I'm no longer writing corporate communications of varying sorts, or developing strategies for a corporation I want to leave, or representing a company I respected, but that stole weekends and evenings as well as the basic ten hours a day I worked there.

I live in Maine.

The first week I lived here I was thrilled to exchange my New Jersey drivers' license for one from Maine. I registered to vote at my new address. And I put Maine license plates on my car. (I still smile when I see those license plates.)

Today, just short of sixteen years later, I'm still excited to be here. I still look out the windows of my home and silently rejoice. I breathe in the salt air. And then I sit down at my desk and get to work.

When I moved to Maine I assumed my sisters and children and all their families would visit often. That hasn't happened. Jobs and marriages and family obligations have taken them further away from Maine. Yes, sometimes they visit. But not often.

But during these years I've married, something I never dreamed of when I moved here, and I've made friends, in person and on line. I'm not lonely. And I love Maine, as I always have. But living here isn't the same as being on vacation.

When I vacationed here I ate seafood every day, and lobsters often. Now I eat lobsters when we have guests, and seafood occasionally. My husband prefers meat, and I don't argue. After all, I used to be the cook. Now he is.

When I vacationed here I went to the beach at least once a summer, went on "tour boats" out of places like Boothbay Harbor, and sat on the rocks at Pemaquid. This year I haven't seen a beach or been out on a boat of any kind, although (when I had guests) I did get to Pemaquid once.

I used to spend days in antique shops and flea markets and at auctions and antique shows. The only antique show I went to this summer was a show I exhibited in. Now I spend my time in libraries and bookstores and art galleries, since my husband is an artist.

When I vacationed here, I got to know mid-coast Maine. Now that I live here as an author I've visited schools and libraries from the southern part of York County to the northern reaches of Aroostook County. I have a much wider picture of the state than I did before.

Before I lived here I'd only made brief visits to Maine in months other than July and August. Now I look forward to seeing autumn colors and ice on the rivers and reflections of snow-covered land in blue water. I know a little bit about wood stoves. (My husband has become an expert.) I have bags of "snakes" to put along window ledges to keep out drafts. My wardrobe leans heavily toward flannel shirts, sweat pants, and wool sweaters. I put Christmas wreaths on all our doors and don't feel guilty about leaving them up until February. (Some people have wreaths on all their doors and windows, and leave them up until April.) I open champagne when the first crocuses appear.

I loved vacationing in Maine. But there is so much more to Maine than Vacationland. Living here 'year 'round? It's the best.

Writing and
The Writing Life

What "Everyone Knows"
About Authors*

*(BUT ISN'T TRUE)

1. All authors are rich.

2. Authors get as many copies of their published books as they want, free, from their publishers. Just ask them — they'll give you one. If they don't give you one, they're not really your friend. (They'd also love to give a copy of their book to any charity that asks. The more giveaways the more readers! And all authors want are readers, right?)

3. Authors get their ideas from a) their dreams, b) the lives of their friends and relatives, c) the daily news and d) complete plots handed to them by strangers. They'd love to hear your ideas for their next book!

4. Authors have plenty of spare time. All they have to do is write down those stories people tell them. So any author would love to a) watch your children; b) walk your dog; c) serve on your organization's board; or d) organize a benefit for your worthy cause and call all his or her writer friends to come and support it. (Remember: they're all rich!)

5. Authors have staffs to take care of their scheduling and itineraries, answer fan letters, keep their mailing lists up-to-date, and do research for their next books. All they have to do is write – their editors take care of the rest.

6. An author may get some rejection slips at first, but after his first book is published, anything he writes will be published.

7. Authors spend a lot of time flying around the country, staying in fancy hotels, being wined and dined, talking with Oprah, and signing their books. The publisher pays for this. If an author is NOT doing this, it's because he's chosen not to.

8. Not all authors smoke, the way they used to, but most of them still drink pretty heavily. Alcohol helps them be creative. They also drink because they're lonely, sitting in front of their computers all the time. Do an author friend a favor by

dropping in unexpectedly several times a week to cheer him up. And bring wine.

9. No matter what they say, authors really are their major characters.

10. Therefore, of course: romance writers have hot sex lives, picture book writers think like first graders, mystery writers want to kill people, and science fiction writers want to blow up the planet. YA authors who write about vampires … well … you can guess. College professors write literary fiction for other college professors to analyze.

11. Authors will be really pleased if you tell them you loved their book so much you loaned your copy to twenty of your best friends. They'll be even more pleased if you tell them that, to save trees, you bought it used on Amazon to begin with.

12. Now that authors can publish their own books, only old-fashioned writers bother working with agents and traditional publishers. They can make a lot more money putting their book up on Kindle themselves. If your author friend doesn't know this, do him a favor by telling him.

Any more questions? Read on, to learn what an author's life is really like …

Time to Write

"If only I had the time, I'd write a book, too …" How many times has every author heard that? And smiled. Because no one ever has enough time.

I wrote my first book (my first mystery – *Shadows at the Fair*) when I was a single parent working full time (ten hour days and on call the rest,) with four children, one grandchild and an elderly parent at home, and occasionally (very occasionally) trying to have a social life.

But writing fiction was what I wanted to do. What I hoped would be my future. That first book was written late at night, early in the morning, on lunch hours, on scraps of paper during boring meetings, on vacations, and in my head, while I was doing everything else. Multitasking can include writing. Agatha Christie once said she got her best ideas while washing the dishes. Long baths and driving work for me.

To be sure, I'm lucky now. My children have their own families. I'm married, and I've left the corporate world behind. For the first time I have a precious "room of my own." But life still creeps in through the telephone and mailbox and email and social networking sites and even through my own body, whose aches and pains remind me that exercise is important and hibernation, unfortunately, works for chipmunks and bears, not for writers. Family is still needy sometimes, friends are important, and, if a writer is lucky enough to have readers — they're important, too.

Research may take months. Marketing books, writing blogs, organizing mailing lists, visiting schools, teaching writing workshops, and speaking at libraries, bookstores and conferences, eats up writing days and weeks.

The joy is that I'm working for myself: living my dream, not someone else's. I love every part of an author's life. My husband does most of our errands and cooking, although since he's become a serious artist we've found our culinary life seriously simplified. And that's okay. Art and words outlast dinners. In the past couple of years we've treated ourselves to the services of a lovely woman who comes every two weeks to give our house what my grandmother would have called "a lick and a promise." She works miracles with a vacuum cleaner, and forces me to keep the house straightened enough so its needs don't pull me away from my desk.

I keep reminding myself that an average book is about 375 pages long. If I write one page a day, a book will be finished in a year. Of course, that doesn't count the research or the fifty or sixty edits BEFORE anyone else sees it.

So I give myself deadlines. Ten pages, or one chapter, a day. Or maybe 25 pages a week. Whatever is challenging, but not totally impossible, to achieve. (The most pages I've written in one day? Thirty-three. Five to ten is much more likely.)

I revise the pages I wrote the day before. Once or twice a month I print out the manuscript and edit the whole mess in hard copy. I do little "things I forgot to check" research tasks along the way. (Yes, it's time consuming, but not doing them drives me crazy – and might open up another plot angle.)

While I'm writing I make notes to remind myself what should have gone before – and what should come afterward.

I read my chapters out loud to pick up inconsistencies, repeated words, and awkward phrases. I revise. I revise again. Writing is a craft. Like all fine crafts, its mastery takes time.

And, ultimately, we all find time for what is most important to us.

Write on!

Where Do Those Ideas
Come From?

I just got home from two weeks on the road.

Yes: a family wedding was included. (A family wedding in Phoenix, I might add. I live in Maine.)

But most of the days I was away from home I was talking about my books — at a children's book festival in Albany, New York, as part of a live variety radio production in New Hampshire, at a mystery bookstore in Scottsdale, Arizona, and at other places along the road, where I smiled, handed out bookmarks, and answered questions.

One of the questions I was asked most often was, "Where do you get your ideas?"

I'm always tempted to say, "I google for them" or "One whole plot came to me in a dream," or "Didn't you know Walmart has an 'ideas section'?"

Of course, I wouldn't say any of those things. But it's hard to explain where ideas come from, because they're everywhere. (Who knows when a wedding in Phoenix might end up in one of my books?)

At least for me, yes, some ideas come from my life. I

probably wouldn't have set books in Maine or New York or New Jersey if I hadn't lived in those places. Or invented a protagonist who was an antique print dealer if I hadn't grown up in a family of antique dealers and collectors. Maggie Summer, my protagonist in the Shadows Antique Print Mystery series, probably wouldn't have thought of becoming a single adoptive parent if I hadn't adopted my four daughters before I was married.

But Maggie is also a college professor. I've never taught. Angie Curtis, the protagonist in my Mainely Needlepoint series, has a license to carry and rarely reads. Not me, in either case.

Often an idea comes from a sentence fragment or a newspaper clipping. If the idea sticks around, I start to dig. Research. Ask more questions. I've written about AIDS (*Shadows at the Fair*) and Alzheimer's (*Shadows on a Maine Christmas.*) I've written about amputation (*Wintering Well*) and rape (*Shadows of a Down East Summer.*) Luckily, I haven't experienced any of those things first hand.

Recently I've written about the politics of lobstering and the embroidery of Mary, Queen of Scots. My information in both cases comes second or third hand — although I have been out on lobster boats, and my Scottish ancestors were Stuarts.

Where do my ideas come from? From life: mine or others. Or from research. Always, they come from digging into a thought, and molding it into a piece of a plot.

Making trouble for my characters.

That's what makes an idea a story.

Which Comes First? Character? Place? Plot? Time?

Perhaps the most difficult question I've ever been asked was from a very serious woman. She'd just finished writing a book, she explained. But she still hadn't decided when her story would take place. "How," she asked me, "How do you decide what period to set your book in?"

That question flummoxed me, as my grandmother would have said, because the woman's question was backwards. How could she have written a story that would ring true — factually, emotionally, sociologically, or geographically — without knowing when (and where) it took place? How could a writer impose a time (or place) on an existing plot?

A story grows out of a specific place and time, even in a basic plot. (Girl loves boy; girl loses boy. Girl finally finds true love.) Characters would have different feelings; different beliefs; different challenges; different possibilities; in different places and years.

Of course, when all the elements of fiction finally come together they become STORY.

But, as someone else asked me, which comes first for an author? Character(s)? Place? Plot? Time?

Another author might have a different answer, but for me, books are built around a place (often small town Maine,) a time (a specific year in a specific century,) and a defining event that either took place or could reasonably have taken place in that time and place. Once I know those elements I can go on to creating my characters (how old are they? what relation do they have to the event? to each other? how does the event change their lives? change them? what do they want? What are they afraid of? What are they hiding? What are they avoiding?)

The plot is how each characters' answers to those questions interact with each other, presenting conflict, challenges, highs, lows, growth for the characters, a crisis or seven, and, finally, an endpoint. In short: action.

Our world changes quickly. For a twentieth century example: the roles of men and women (and their relationships to each other) have changed decisively during the past sixty years. A woman who grew up in the nineteen fifties wouldn't see her world, her potential, her future, in the same way as a woman who grew up in the nineteens sixties or seventies. Certainly not in the way a young woman of today would.

And the men who grew up next to those women also saw the world differently — differently from the woman, and differently in every decade.

Move those two people back a century – or two – or more — and their worlds are even more different. Not just the physical worlds in which they live and tasks they must do, but their goals. What has changed most is their view of the world, and of their place in it. Of course, where those people live (what country? what region? state? city or town or farm?) and their race, and their socio-economic status are also critical elements to defining them.

Today many people take anti-depressants or anti-anxiety pills to help them get through their days. In the nineteenth century they took opium, or laudanum (a mixture of opium and alcohol.) What alcohol would they have drunk? Gin, for lower glasses in the Great Britain. Beer, for early Europeans in America. Sherry, for wealthy nineteenth century women who weren't prohibitionists. Whiskey and/or beer for Irish immigrants. Cocktails, in the 1920s.

Class differences; geographic differences; whether you were a man or a woman; all changed the way you accepted or rejected the idea of drinking alcohol.

And so forth.

So, what comes first? For me, a place. A time. A challenge or event or circumstance. Then the characters appear. Characters who have grown up in that time or place, or have for some reason (why?) come to that place. Characters who must cope with the demands of their time. Characters who are in conflict with parts of themselves, or with others.

Only when all of those are in place can plotting begin.

How to Write a Cozy Mystery

So, you want to write a mystery? You don't know too much about police procedures, or regulations for private detectives, or the law, but you enjoy settling in with a good book in which the bad guys are caught and the good guys (and gals) win out in the end?

Writing a mystery might just be your cup of tea.

Or thimble of arsenic.

Why not try? Traditional mysteries, also known as cozies, are in the Agatha Christie tradition where, it's often said, "more tea is spilled than blood." They've been popular for decades, and, despite today's increased popularity of suspense and thrillers, are still selling well.

Their readers and authors are predominantly, but not exclusively, women. They even have their own conference, Malice Domestic, held each spring just outside of Washington, D.C., and their own awards: the Agathas, named after you-know-who.

The first book in my Shadows Antique Print Mystery series, *Shadows at the Fair*, was lucky enough to be a finalist for a "best first mystery" Agatha, forever giving me a place in the traditional mystery world. And I've written

ten more cozies since then, so I have some qualifications to give advice about the genre.

The protagonist of the cozy is usually a woman. She's not a law-enforcement professional, although she may have a friend who is. She's a moderately idiosyncratic adult female who lives a full and active life, has an interesting profession or hobby, and has at least one (preferably more) unresolved personal issue in her life. (An ex-husband who's a pain, a difficult child, an alcoholic parent, a secret past. Anything of this sort will do.)

Most important, she has an amazing ability to be in a place where others are murdered — and to always have a logical and justifiable reason to get involved in solving the crime herself. (A friend of hers is accused of the murder? The body is on her property? The victim is a business associate? Or former beau?)

Those are the basic components of the cozy. The author (you) still can't ignore basic rules regarding the relationship between busy-bodies (that's your protagonist) and law enforcers. You can't invent forensics, whether CSI does or not. There are books to help you, or, ideally, you can consult with someone in your local police force. State laws vary. And if your case involves the Feds, you'll need to get that straight. Your readers take their mysteries seriously. They'll know the rules, and you'd better, too. There's no excuse for not doing your research homework.

You'll need at least three, but no more than six, possible suspects for your murder or murders. (Two murders are better than one, but don't wipe out the whole town. You'll need some characters left for the next book in the series.)

Each suspect should have MOM. (A mother is fine, and can even complicate the plot, but in this case we're talking Motive, Opportunity, and Means.) Your sleuth's job is to unravel all of that.

Although a book with a professional crime fighter as protagonist often opens with a body being found, a traditional mystery usually involves you with the characters first. The first murder occurs perhaps 20-30% of the way through the book.

The murder is not described in detail, nor is any sex that might occur. (Your protagonist doesn't have to be celibate, but she – and most cozy protagonists are women — does have to draw the shades.)

If you want to add a second murder, about 60-70% of the way through the book is a good place for that to happen. It also helps keep the middle of the book going, just about the time you and your readers are feeling a bit bored.

You'll need an action scene at the end, during which your protagonist will confront the villain, put herself in danger, and, of course the murderer will be caught and all dangling plot ends will be tied off. This should happen very close to the end of the book — a few pages before you turn off your computer.

One more thing. No matter what, no cats or dogs or children must die. Although a cat would be a good addition to your cast.

Now you're ready. I've shared all the secrets. All you have to do is write the book.

Beginning a New Series

In a day or two I'll be starting to write the first book of a new series.

And I'll admit I'm nervous.

It isn't as though the book won't find a home. I'm lucky to already have a contract with Kensington for a three-book series.

It isn't as though I've never done this before. I've written seven books in my *Shadows Antique Print Mystery* series.

It's not even as though I have no ideas for this new book, or series. It even has a (tentative) name: *Twisted Threads*. It has a location (Haven Harbor, Maine, somewhere near Cabot Cove.) It has a protagonist (Angie Curtis, age 28,) and her partner, (Margaret Curtis, Angie's grandmother, aged 65.) It has a background thread …. stitchery, especially needlepoint. (Angie and her grandmother create custom needlepoint and appraise and preserve antique stitchery.)

It even has a beginning …

"The day had already been the sort you want to drown in a cold beer or a bubble bath. Preferably both. And that was

before I heard Gram's voice, loud and clear as always, coming from my "missed messages."

"Angel, it's time to come home. They've found your mama."

No one in Arizona called me "Angel."

So — why am I nervous? Because beginning a new book (especially one that's the start of a new series) is fraught with decisions I haven't made. What month is it? What's the time span of the book? How much time will pass between this book and the next in the series? How much romance will there be? How many suspects will there be who might be responsible for the two murders I plan to include?

I've done most of the necessary research. I have ideas. I feel as though I'm planning to attend a party I know will be filled with new people. I have my invitation. I have my dress. But I don't know the people who will be there. And it's going to be a long party.

Yes, I'm looking forward to going. I'm hopeful I'll have a wonderful time. But, yes, I'm a little nervous.

And I hope you'll be there with me, when *Twisted Threads* is published.

Visiting Grandma in Maine – When Grandma is an Author

Like most of us, I wear several hats. I'm a mystery author. I'm a children's author. To my family I'm a wife, mother of four, and grandma to eight.

So far as most of my family is concerned, I'm retired. After all, I don't get up five days a week, put on a suit and heels, and carry a briefcase to a corporate office the way I did for (and this is the sad truth) thirty years.

It's frustrating when children and grandchildren don't understand that writing is my new job; that sometimes I have to say "no" when a deadline or speaking obligation keeps me from a family event.

So when two of my grandchildren, ages ten and eleven, asked to spend three weeks with my husband and me this summer, we decided to say, "Yes – but some days we'll have to work." We knew we couldn't do much, if any, painting or writing while they visited, but it would be an opportunity to give Vanessa and Samantha a glimpse of the lives we live: the daily lives of an author and artist.

So, three weeks ago, they flew to Maine from rural

Virginia. Since then they've been to Pemaquid Beach, shopped for sweatshirts in Boothbay Harbor, eaten lobsters and mussels and s'mores, and watched "really old" VHS and DVD movies from my library (most from the 1980s and 90s,) just as I'm sure thousands of other children visiting grandparents in Maine have done this July.

They loved visiting the Coastal Maine Botanical Gardens and making ice cream and eating blueberry pancakes and staying up later than their usual bedtimes.

They also test-cooked recipes for the popovers and cream puffs and pizza that are part of a contemporary mystery for children I've written that hasn't yet sold. (They made some excellent suggestions on clarifying the instructions.)

They went with me to a signing at a jail built in 1811 featured in *Finest Kind*, one of my historical novels for young people. ("A really scary place. Gross that prisoners had to pee in buckets.") They hung out at a couple of bookstore signings. ("Why weren't there lines of people here like at the jail?")

We tucked a trip to Acadia National Park into a trip to the library in Bar Harbor, where I spoke (along with Julia Spencer Fleming and Vicki Doudera) about writing mysteries. They sat very quietly for the ninety minute evening presentation. On our walk back to the motel we listened to a band concert on the village green and afterward, one of them, looking into a dark alley, asked, "Is that the kind of place you'd find a body?"

We went to openings at two galleries where my husband shows his art. We visited the Farnsworth Museum, where they chose posters for their rooms at home. (One Jamie Wyeth and one Robert Indiana: both Maine artists.)

At home, Vanessa, for the first time, asked if she could have her own copy of *Stopping to Home*, one of my books for young people, to read, and I autographed one for her. Reading is hard for Vanessa, but she's now up to page 74. I'm (quietly) thrilled.

In our spare time I've also been teaching the girls to build bookcases. The results aren't perfect, but we now have two finished, and one in progress. There are bookcases in every room of my house, and these are for our back upstairs hall, to hold an overflow of middle grade and YA novels.

As they helped me re-shelve books (alphabetically, of course) they recognized books they'd read, and books by authors they'd met, and each chose a couple of books to take home to read later. We talked about books they'd seen the movie versions of, and why the movies might be different from the books.

We read a lot of Harry Potter in the three weeks they were here, and saw several of the movies, courtesy of Netflix.

Vanessa and Sam are flying home tomorrow, and will start the fifth and sixth grades next Tuesday. I'll miss them. I hope they had a memorable Maine vacation. I also hope the next time we talk on the telephone, or see each other on Skype, that they'll understand a little better what Grandma and Grandpa do in Maine.

No, we don't leave home every morning to work in offices, like their mom and dad do.

But we have jobs, just the same.

Polishing

I'm writing this from "Writers' Jail." That's what my friend and fellow author Barbara Ross calls it when your manuscript deadline is fast approaching, and you're behind schedule. Your editor's schedule or your schedule … it doesn't matter how you figure it. You know it when it happens. The only sane response is to lock yourself away, cancel all social engagements, hand your spouse the shopping list, and close your study door. (And when you're in there? Turn off the internet and write. Don't forget that part.)

So… I'm in writers' jail, with a manuscript due in two months. That sounds like oodles of time left … except for the appearances I've agreed to do (and refuse to cancel) and the guests who will be visiting. And the one hundred pages, more or less, I still have to write on my first draft. Not to speak of time for editing.

So what was I doing this morning?

Polishing brass. I have a lot of brass and copper in my house, and quite a bit of silver, too. I inherited some, I was given some, and some I bought in Calcutta. Like most "things" in my home, most of these objects have histories.

141

Like – the brass lamp made from a shell one of my grandmother's brothers brought back from World War I.

But I digress.

Despite those who speak of "patina" as a justification to ignore dirt, grime, and tarnish, I firmly believe copper, brass and silver needs to be polished at least every six months. Brass and copper can go twelve months if it's a really rough year, but silver needs loving care or bad things will happen. And silver is not only a joy, but an investment.

So, because I am guilty of setting quarterly goals, I include polishing on my "to do" list every other quarter. This year that was to be the first quarter. But life, and an earlier manuscript deadline, and publicity for my April book, meant that although I polished most of the silver, I only got to a few pieces of brass and copper. (I generally move from room to room. The living room with the brass fireplace set, including fire dogs, tools, screen and fender tends to be the last room on my list.)

Now, when I'm at this panicked point in a manuscript I usually aim at writing at least ten pages a day. Sometimes I can do more. Sometimes less. But ten pages is a heavy writing day.

Even when I'm in the depths of those pages, though, I need to take breaks.

Eye breaks. (Look out the window! Don't you wish you were there, outside?)

Stretching breaks. (Even ergonomic keyboards don't help with ten pages. Not to speak of when you have a cat on your lap.)

Tea breaks. (Self-explanatory.)

Sometimes, in desperation, chocolate breaks.

And polishing breaks.

Paths of Research …
Diderot and Me

I write historical novels for young people as well as mysteries for adults, so I'm very familiar with researching the past.

Even for my contemporary *Shadows Antique Print Mystery* series I have to do historical research. For example, in *Shadows of a Down East Summer* I wrote an "1890 diary" of one of the young women who posed for Winslow Homer that summer. It was great fun recreating Prouts Neck, Maine at that time.

In *Thread and Gone*, in my Mainely Needlepoint series, I managed to connect Mary, Queen of Scots, to Marie Antoinette … and to Maine.

In my Shadows series I include information about antique prints and the artists, engravers, lithographers and publishers who produced them. Although I've been an antique print dealer since 1977, I still check everything to make sure I have the dates and information correct.

My Mainely Needlepoint series includes details about needlepoint and embroidery done in the past.

This summer I've been writing *Shadows on a Maine Christmas.*

Of course, my heroine, Maggie Summer, is going to give her beau and his aunt antique prints Christmas morning. I knew she would give Aunt Nettie prints to match the Morris birds I'd hung on Nettie's wall in an earlier book. But for Will?

I thought for a while, and then happened to glance around my study. On my study wall I have a framed page from Diderot's Encyclopedia called *L'Art D'Ecrire* (The art of writing.)

Denis Diderot (1713-1784) was a French philosopher and writer, and editor of the *Encyclopedia Systematic: Dictionary of the Sciences, Arts and Crafts by a Company of Men of Letters* published between 1765 and 1772. It wasn't the first encyclopedia — that was written by Ephraim Chambers in England. But Diderot's twenty seven folio volumes were far more ambitious than Chamber's volumes were, and included numerous engravings illustrating various arts and crafts.

Maggie's guy, Will Brewer, used to teach woodworking in a high school, and now is an antique dealer specializing in fireplace and kitchen wares. So what page or pages in Diderot's encyclopedia might Maggie give him to hang on the walls of HIS study? I didn't have any in my collection, but I knew they must exist.

I started googling and, indeed, found another print dealer who had a number of pages from the encyclopedia. Among them were pictures of carpentry tools, and barrel making, and the making of fish nets. Perfect. Just what Maggie should give Will for his Maine study.

In the process, I discovered that my *L'Art D'Ecrire* was one of sixteen full-page prints, part of a section of forty three pages in the encyclopedia that described writing. My print shows a man writing at a desk. Another in the encyclopedia pictures a woman writing, and several other pages illustrate how to hold a pen, make a quill pen, and how to make ink. Different forms of calligraphy make up the rest of the section.

Further searches told me that in 1956 Hermes designer Maurice Trenchant created an elegant silk scarf for the famous up-scale company based on the Diderot *L'Art D'Ecrire* pages. Very cool! Additional searches also found a Hermes jacket based on the same pages. The scarf was re-issued in 1998-1999, so any collector (I now knew people collected Hermes scarves as decorative objects, not just as wearing apparel) would have to beware and identify which edition of the scarf they were purchasing.

And, in case you're interested in acquiring such a scarf, on-line sources priced it at $500 and up.

A simple search for an eighteenth century print had taken me into the world of high-priced fashion today. I also found (who could stop now?) that actress Kelly Rutherford had worn one of these coveted scarves in season one of the television program *Gossip Girl* (a show I've never watched.)

Which is exactly why I love doing research. (And why sometimes it's hard to stop.)

Creating a Character Bible

A character bible is a writing tool I develop for each book I write. I find it important for stand-alone books — and indispensable for a series.

No; I'm not referring to THE Bible.

I'm referring to a place — a notebook, an electronic file, a folder, whatever you choose, that contains the important facts about the people and places in your book. Who wants a character to change eye colors between chapters two and twenty?

Everyone has to find their own "best way" to create a useful bible. I've found a hand-written loose leaf notebook is easiest for me. I can update it by hand either while I'm writing or after. I can refer to it easily. And I can add (or subtract) pages when necessary. Some years ago I treated myself to a leather notebook. It's a comfortable size to take with me if I'm writing on the road, 6.5 x 8.5 inches, and I love the way it looks and feels. Since I use it all the time, I think of it as an investment.

At the moment it contains information about the people and places in both my Shadows Antique Print Mystery series and my Mainely Needlepoint Series.

What's in there? Maps of the major towns where the books are set: Haven Harbor and Weymouth, Maine, and the campus where Maggie Summer teaches in New Jersey. If another town appears in a book I also draw a map, but usually I leave those maps in the folder of back-up information (research, ideas, outline, etc.) I keep for each book.

Most of my bible is made up of alphabetical listings of information about each character. A character who only appears in one book may have a short listing — how old he or she is, what they look like, specific quirks they have, what their secret is, what they want, and what they're willing to do to get it, and perhaps their relation to my series protagonist and the specific plot line.

In a mystery, if they're either murdered or the murderer, that may be all I need — they'll only appear in one, or maybe two, books.

For major, repeating, characters, I include not only that basic information but other details.

For instance, my bible tells me Maggie Summer (in the Shadows series) has never smoked, drinks Diet Pepsi, and loves chocolate covered cherries. She pays high taxes on her house in New Jersey. She drinks Dry Sack sherry out of Edinburgh Crystal. She likes to treat herself to baths with lavender-scented soap. Her father took her deer hunting when she was thirteen but she refused to shoot, even though he'd taught her how to use a gun. She cried when he killed a doe. (He never took her hunting again.) And so forth

Angie Curtis, the protagonist of the Mainely Needlepoint series? Her Gram calls her "Angel." She has a birthmark on her shoulder that matches one her mother had. She has scars on her toes from walking on barnacle-covered rocks as a child. She drives a small red Honda, likes her coffee black, and is pretty flexible about her choice of beers – but prefers those made in Maine.

Gussie White reads late at night, so it's okay to call her then. Aunt Nettie has a Thursday morning appointment every week at Cut 'n' Curl. Angie Curtis' fashion-plate friend Clem Walker was fat as a teenager and now works for Channel 7 in Portland.

Not all those details appear in all my books, but they've been mentioned in at least one. The real purpose of the bible is to ensure that my words don't contradict themselves. I don't want Maggie eating chocolate covered cherries in one book and being allergic to cherries in another. (If I don't notice, one of my readers definitely will.)

The character bible is also the place to include backstories, phobias, hair styles, fears and goals.

In addition to characters, I have pages for specific places — Harbor Haunts, a restaurant in Haven Harbor, has red Formica counters. Maggie Summer's kitchen table is pine. What kind of trees are on the main street of town? What do characters' houses look like? How far away are local hospitals, and how long does it take to drive there? All details that may be important in more than one book.

When do I put information in my bible? I used to

create or add information when I was planning my book. But although I do a general outline of each book before I start writing, I tend to change details as I write. So, for me, the time to create my bible is when I've finished a strong draft, or when I send the manuscript to my editor.

Having the bible helps avoid changing a character's hair color, or height, or the name of his or her ex-spouse. It's also a convenient place to check that I haven't created two characters with the same first name (ouch! yes, that's happened) or even two characters with similar last names. I try, in fact, to have all character names in one book start with different letters. That makes it easier for readers to keep them straight. (Me, too.)

Reading through the bible not only makes sure I don't make continuity mistakes, it also gives me ideas for future plots, and doesn't let me forget minor characters who might have key roles to play in future books.

I keep it right next to my thesaurus and dictionary on my desk.

It is essential.

Stealing Words

I am a thief.

I steal words.

I'm stealthy. I don't steal more than one, or possibly two, at a time, so tracing their origins would be impossible, even for me.

I steal them from friends and relatives and CNN commentators. I reach out and boldly snatch them from overheard conversations at grocery stores or farmers' markets or coffee shops. But, worse of all, most of the words I've stolen have come from those in my own profession. I steal them from other writers.

I steal them for the same reason a jeweler might steal a jewel: they are so beautiful I can't resist taking them and making them my own.

I carry a notebook, as most writers do, and that's where I capture those precious, fleeting, words. Often they are sensory words. Images. Words I recognize, I admire, but that I don't always use myself. Or that I suddenly see, or hear, in a different way. That remind me of smells or sights or tastes that fit in scenes in the book I'm writing.

They are treasures. I hoard them.

I copy them onto lists and I read them over, cherishing the way they feel, before writing or rewriting a certain scene, or before starting my work for the day. They evoke feelings. Memories. They are almost a meditation. Sometimes they form themselves into short phrases.

What are some of the words and phrases on my list now?

Sea lavender, wishing stones, frayed, wafted, cobalt blue, gray skeletal pilings, the scent of lavender in an old pine bureau, the front of a house painted white while the back is wind-grayed, socked in, glowing, fingers grazing, skittered, slog, fragile, mud and mold and rotting fish, screams of fishers in the dark, creak of hardwood boards, shabby, clamoring

And many more. Some of them will no doubt end up finding homes in my book. Or the one after that. Some will not. But reading them over will remind me why I love writing. Words are my tools.

Go ahead.

I dare you.

Steal some of mine.

Words are magic. Used by different authors, they tell different stories. And yet, standing alone, or in limited company, they contain their own messages. They sing their own songs.

"Warning! Adult Book!"
In the Eyes of the Beholder

Since I write in two genres, at book events focusing solely on books for adults or solely books for children, I often find myself the only author wearing two hats. That's what happened last weekend.

While it felt as though most of the mystery writers in the United States were at Bouchercon, the World Mystery Convention, I was in the little town of Warwick, New York, at a children's book festival with fifty other authors and illustrators of books for children.

Typical of such gatherings, most of the attendees were teachers, librarians, and parents with children under the age of ten. The youngest attendees happily picked out books about trucks, baseball, dinosaurs, princesses and pink birthday parties. Older children were clearly either a) addicted to reading, or b) dragged by a parent.

The most popular author in the room? No contest. The one who'd brought a giant Madagascar Hissing Cockroach in a cage for "show and tell." How could any mere book compete with live action?

I write historicals for ages eight and up. Maryrose Wood, who sat next to me, also writes "middle grade" books, as they're known in the trade. Across from us was an author who wrote YA titles with dark covers. Most of our customers were librarians and teachers.

With the exception of one book.

Those ordering books for the festival had, in addition to my books for children, ordered (in error? I didn't ask) copies of my latest mystery. It sat on my table, apart from my historicals, behind a large "ADULT BOOK" sign. *Shadows of a Down East Summer* might not include any on-camera violence or sex … (I suspect some of the YA books in the room contained more of both) but *it was not written for children.* In this room of books about piglets and airplanes that talked, this book was clearly "R" rated.

Time and again children, usually aged 11-14, picked it up, sometimes surreptitiously, and begged their parents to buy it. And, bless their parents, most of the time they won. One young lady whispered that she'd like me to sign her copy to "Detective Sarah, please," because she was going to be a detective when she grew up.

A man, overhearing me discussing the book with a parent, interrupted to ask, "But would your book be appropriate for a forty-year-old?"

I assured him it would.

"Good," he said. "I'll take one. My wife and I like children's books like yours."

He winked as I signed his book.

I hope both he and Detective Sarah enjoyed their

purchases.

I remember being about twelve, and feeling very grownup (and a bit sneaky) when I managed to elude the librarian and settle into my favorite window seat at my local town library and devour science fiction and mysteries shelved on the second floor — in the *adult* department.

Funny thing. By the time I was old enough to take those books home (legally), I'd moved on. Mysteries and science fiction no longer interested me. Maybe I'd been fascinated with them because they were forbidden.

I hope those, of all ages, who bought *Shadows of a Down East Summer* at Warwick last weekend enjoy it. And that they continue to seek out books that have enticing labels and covers.

It's not the only way to discover new worlds. But it's a beginning. And no book should ever be forbidden.

Signing that book

Before my first book was published I thought of a book signing as a somewhat mystical event. I went to quite a few of the New York City YMHA readings by literary figures and sat in awe of my own personal gods and goddesses (Toni Morrison! Louise Erdrich! Michael Dorris! Alice Walker!)

I owned all their books. But I never dared bother them by joining the lines to have those books signed. It seemed so – presumptuous.

Luckily, most readers are not as intimidated as I was.

And when first faced with a real, actual, book of my own, I was suddenly overwhelmed by decisions. Does one sign on the title page? The dedication page? The blank page at the front of the book? I asked other authors, and found they had very strong – and different – opinions. (I decided to sign on the title page.)

On last week's episode of the television program *Castle* I was horrified to see "Richard Castle" sign his latest best seller *on the cover*. "No!" I wanted to shriek. "It will smear! No one signs *on the cover!*"

Since some of my books are for children, I frequently

sign books for young readers. At my first children's book fair I became incredibly jealous when I saw author/illustrators drawing little pictures next to their signatures. The first time a child asked me to sign a book and then examined my signature to see whether I'd drawn a roller-skating dinosaur or a teddy bear or, best of all, a portrait of HER — and found I'd just signed my name … it was sad. "I just write books," I had to explain lamely. "I don't draw."

Some authors, I was advised, develop a special signing signature, different from their real signature, for legal reasons. (So no one can forge their name.) Since my legal name is not Lea Wait (didn't know that, did you?) luckily, I didn't have that problem.

Which brings up the all-important choice of pen. Ball point looks so … common. But nothing that smears … And ink color. Black? Blue? Brown? And width of point …

And of course you must write a memorable phrase in addition to your name. "Happy reading!" is not sizzling. "We must have been lovers in another life" would attract attention, but possibly not the attention you'd want. I settled, in my first book, for "May you have a lifetime filled with happy endings." It worked for almost anyone, and took a while to write — which was great when you didn't have a lot of people waiting in line for your signature. (My publicist had told me it was good to slow down the line so you always looked busy.)

I've had fourteen books published now. I've had short

lines and long lines. I've written memorable notes and had people come back ten minutes later and say, hesitantly, "Excuse me, but what did you write? I can't read your handwriting."

I figure I'm an expert.

So, tonight, I'm going to speak at a library and do a signing. I have my special pens ready, and my useful words in mind. I know what page to sign on.

If you buy one of my books, please ask me to sign it. No author will ever feel it's an imposition. Trust me. Now I know.

Visiting Schools

Part of writing for children is visiting classrooms and being part of children's literature festivals: venues where I get to talk with young readers, share information about my books and how I write them, talk about what an author's life is like, run writing workshops, and, most of all, answer questions.

I've spoken with kindergarteners and college seniors in fourteen states, but because I write "middle grade" books, most often I speak to students in grades four through eight. And when it comes time for questions, I always begin by saying no subject is off-limits.

Some teachers flinch when I say that, but so far I haven't died of embarrassment, and neither have they.

To many children, the author of a book they've read is a celebrity. At one school I was signing in at the office when I saw two young ladies, noses pressed against the glass in the lobby. One said to the other, "Is the author here?" "Nope," replied the other. "I haven't seen any limos pull in yet."

I always carry postcards of my latest book, which I autograph for students; otherwise I'm asked to autograph notebooks, scraps of paper, book covers, and arms. (I don't sign body parts.)

I'm often asked if I know J.K. Rowling. Or Stephen King. Or Stephanie Meyers. Or Rick Riordan. (When I actually HAVE met someone on their dream list — like Stephen King, or Rick Riordan — they stare in awe.)

Only once was I caught without an answer to a question. I was being interviewed by a seventh grade reporter on a morning CCTV program at a middle school in Missouri. He asked me, "What is your favorite word?" For the life of me I couldn't think of a response. And we were on the air! I asked for another question. Then I went back to the first one and answered. My favorite word, I'd decided, was "hope."

I was asked the same question later that month in Pennsylvania, so it must have been in the air that spring.

What do children want to know? The same things adults want to know, but often don't ask.

How old am I? (68.) How old was I when my first book was published? (53. Yes; old.) What did I have for breakfast? Well, maybe adults aren't so interested in that one. Luckily, the first time I was asked I'd had oatmeal and orange juice. Parents, it seems, tell their darlings that 'smart people eat good breakfasts', and the kids figure an author must be smart, so they're checking to see if their parents were right.

How long does it take you to write a book? (Three to six months to research an historical, which my published books for young people are; three to five months to write it; two months to edit it. Less time for a contemporary.)

Do you use Wikipedia? (Rarely, and I always check any "facts" there.)

Why is the boy on the hard cover edition of *Wintering Well* different from the boy on the paperback edition? (Different editors.) Doesn't the author get to choose the covers? (No. And I don't like that other cover either.)

What are the names of your children? Well, then what are the names of your grandchildren? (Real question: do any of them have MY name.)

Once a young man stared at a necklace I was wearing and finally blurted out, "Is that a diamond?" I told him that, alas, it was a quartz crystal. But we agreed the quartz was pretty anyway.

I've been told I don't look like my author photo. I've been asked to write a book about the town/class/person asking the question. (I tell them they should write it; they know their subject better than I do.) I've been told secrets, either between classes or in passed notes or during the luncheons teachers sometimes arrange between a few students and the visiting author. Often the secret is that the child is adopted, since they know I've adopted children. Sometimes the secret is that they want to be a writer. Or that they don't like to read, but they liked my book anyway. Or that their mom has a boyfriend, so that's why they read a lot of books at the library.

A young man in the mid-west asked me for advice. He was living with his grandmother because both his parents were in prison, but his dad was getting out soon and he was afraid his dad would take him away so he'd never see his mom again. He was keeping a journal that he hoped his grandmother would give to his mother if he disappeared so she'd know he loved her. He wondered if I thought that was a good idea. I told him I thought it was a very good idea, but also suggested he share his fears with his social worker. I don't know if he did, or what happened to him. Sometimes it feels safe to share a secret with someone you'll probably never see again.

In Maine I spoke to an English as a second language class of fifth graders who'd read my *Seaward Born*. One young man from Somalia was very restless, and finally could contain himself no longer. He waved his hand frantically. "Lady, lady? How much money you make?" he called out. I explained that if he bought the hard cover of the book he'd read, I'd get $1.70. If he bought the paperback, I'd get about fifty cents.

He thought about that for a moment. Then his hand shot up again. "Lady, lady! You looking for new job, soon?"

An intelligent young man, to be sure.

That same class, having heard that I adopted older children who came to this country not speaking English, also had questions about that. ("How long before they speak good English?" "Did they marry people from their country or from America?" "Did they have same names at school and at home?" "Did they go to college?" "Do they have good jobs now?" "Did they miss their country very bad?") Answering those questions for a little while was more important than talking about my book.

I've had sixth and seventh grade students shyly hand me inch thick manuscripts of the novels they were working on. I tell them I don't have time to read them, but I suggest critique groups, or, in some cases, writers' conferences in the area, or writers' groups I know of, and writers' magazines.

I make sure their teachers know about their books. A few years ago, inspired by Harry Potter and other fantasy adventures, most young people were writing fantasies. Now, with the success of *The Hunger Games* and other dystopian literature, I hear more about futuristic books. A few young Danielle Steeles are focused on romances.

These are the young people who ask me about how to get published. How to get an agent. Whether they should self-publish or not. Some of them have surprisingly sophisticated questions.

My advice to any author who's never visited a school is simple: never underestimate students, of any age, and never talk down to them. Let the students lead the way. You may be surprised at some of their questions, but you can be sure they're serious. And there's nothing more important than answering the questions of the next generation of readers, and writers. We owe them our best.

I wish I'd had the chance to meet "a really, truly, author" when I was their age.

This is My Life — and My Study

People often ask writers what their writing habits or schedules are.

My schedule isn't as set as those of many writers. Research, plotting, marketing, and taking time to be with family and friends all take hours and days away from actual writing time. But I do work on my writing in some way every day, seven days a week, 365 days a year.

About seven years ago, for the first time in my life, I got my own study. That's where I spend most of my life now. I designed it the way I'd always dreamed my study would be, and although sometimes I wish it were a little bigger, most of the time it's just perfect.

A room filled with my "sometimes used" reference books is down the hall, but my study has room for the wide assortment of dictionaries I use often, a bookcase full of books of names, atlases, references for the book I'm currently writing, press clippings and reviews, nineteenth century texts I take when I visit schools, file cabinets holding manuscripts in waiting, and folders full of ideas for future books.

I converted a nineteenth century wardrobe to hold

office supplies. On my desk are other essentials, like the ceramic pencil holder my daughter Elizabeth made in high school that I keep filled with sharply pointed pencils, even though I do 90% of my writing on a computer. I just like having the pencils there.

Other necessities? A mug of Tootsie Roll Pops, for encouragement and solace, in case a plot needs a little more contemplation. My appointment calendar for this year and next. A wooden file card holder where I can arrange (and rearrange) my plots.

Next to my desk is a small bar-sized refrigerator full of bottles of cold water. On top is an electric kettle, so I can make an emergency cup of tea. That comes in especially handy on cold Maine winter afternoons, since my study is on the second floor, far from our kitchen.

Several inspirational items hang above my desk: a small oil portrait of Edgar Allen Poe my husband bought for me at an auction, my Agatha nominations, a lifetime achievement award in literature from the college I attended, a button reading "Another Deadline, Another Miracle," and the arrow of a 19th century iron weathervane, pointing up, which I hope is the direction my career will take.

On my desk there's a small brass statue of Lakshmi, the Hindu goddess of prosperity, which I brought back from Calcutta, and a framed picture of a rainbow over our barn.

Other good luck pieces include a tiny glass iron that a friend of my great-grandmother threw to her as she stood on the deck of the ship taking her from Wales to Boston in 1880 to marry a man she'd never met. A carved stone face my mother found on a beach in Maine. A piece of sea-glass in the shape of a gull. Several heart-shaped sea-stones. My sterling silver baby mug, complete with tooth marks, holding paper clips.

All props to set the stage.

What does my typical day look like?

I'm not a morning person, so unless I have a tight deadline I don't write then. Usually after a cup of tea and some oatmeal with blueberries or raisins I post about the Maine Crime Writers blog on Facebook, answer my email, and take care of any necessary marketing or accounting tasks. Often those chores take me a good part of the morning. My artist husband, who has likely been up since before dawn and painted for several hours before breakfast (he IS a morning person,) is probably still in his studio in our ell, or out doing errands while I'm doing that.

Late in the morning he makes lunch, we'll take a break to eat and watch the news, and then, while he takes an after-lunch siesta, I'll start writing.

On a good day I'll write until 5 or 6 o'clock, when he'll suggest it might be time for a glass of wine. If I'm ready to stop, I will. If not, we'll delay dinner for another hour or so. .

Sometimes after dinner I'll go back and edit, or finish a scene. Sometimes I'll check email or Facebook again; sometimes I'll read or watch television.

There's a pad and pencil next to my bed in case any word or phrase or solution to a writing problem pops up while I'm doing something else, including sleeping. And it all starts again the next day.

When I'm under a tight deadline I write all day, email and accounting chores get less attention, and my mind moves further away from home and closer to wherever my plot leads me. My amazingly patient husband knows when those times are, and has been known to silently place a cup of tea on the side of my desk, take telephone messages, and generally act as a guardian for my frazzled world. He knows when he asks me a question and I don't respond, or answer with a blank look, that it isn't personal.

He's also more relieved than I am when that phase of writing is over and we can celebrate another completed book with champagne and hope and send it winging off.

And I can begin again.

When Storms Come In …

(Note: This essay originally appeared in Volume 30, Number 2, (2014,) of *Mystery Readers Journal.*)

One of the challenges of writing a mystery is keeping the hero or heroine on their toes. No matter what happens, they need to be thrown obstacle after obstacle to overcome until finally they succeed in identifying the killer and put the universe on an even keel once again.

Obstacles take many forms. Suspects who have motives and opportunity can lead the sleuth in the wrong direction. Personal problems – physical, emotional, or relationship – can be distracting. Life can interfere, in the guise of a flat tire or flood or fire or, as in two of my books, *Shadows of a Down East Summer* and *Shadows on a Cape Cod Wedding*, the interference may be severe storms. In both cases weather complicates the protagonist's life, and therefore delays the resolution of the plot.

In *Shadows of a Down East Summer* a Maine nor'easter arrives on the day of an antique show scheduled to be held outdoors on a county fair ground. My protagonist, Maggie Summer, like me, is an antique print dealer who refuses to do outdoor shows because of the damage winds, rain and dust can do to prints. But her beau, Will Brewer, specializes in kitchen ware and fireplace implements. He has no problem with outdoor shows.

I've attended many outdoor antiques shows, and have exhibited at shows where my booth was safely indoors, but others were outside, under tents. So I was all too familiar with the problems Maggie and Will faced when they got up pre-dawn to drive to a fairground to set up for a one-day show and discover the road partially washed out, the fairground awash in mud, and tents teetering in high winds and heavy rains. Eventually making it to the spot where they're going to set up, they must keep their antiques dry while moving them from the van to their booth under the tent. The tent quakes and shudders. Breaks in the tent stitching results in sudden inside downpours, soaking merchandise not designed to be used outdoors. The tent poles sink deeper in the mud, while the tent itself, caught by the winds, threatens to collapse or sail off. Maggie and Will are soaked and cold. And, of course, few customers arrive.

Just one more day in the reality of antique dealing.

And their absence from home dealing with the storm means than an event crucial to the mystery's plot can happen while they are out defying the elements.

Several dozen antique dealers told me that my description of antique dealers coping with the storm was their favorite part of the book. They, too, had put the legs of mahogany tables in soup cans to keep them away from mud, and attempted in vain to keep textiles and paintings dry in torrential downpours.

The storm worked so well, in fact, that in *Shadows on a Cape Cod Wedding* I created a late-season hurricane which hit the Cape in October. Airports were closed, keeping wedding guests from afar from arriving. Bridges were shut, roads were flooded, the wedding reception venue was under water, and electrical power was out, so food couldn't be cooked.

The storm complicated life for everyone, good and bad, on the Cape.

And of course my villain took advantage of the storm to … But, then, if I told you, you wouldn't read the book!

I wrote *Shadows on a Cape Cod Wedding* before Hurricane Sandy hit the New England Coast in 2012. I based the storm in the book on a hurricane I remembered: Hurricane Carol. I was a child, vacationing on the Cape with my family, in 1954 when Hurricane Carol threatened to come ashore. I remember us packing up quickly and being evacuated on the one road that leaves the Cape and crosses the bridge to the mainland and which was jammed with traffic. We later heard the cottage we'd rented that summer had been flooded up to the second floor.

Since then I've lived through a wide assortment of hurricanes. I've watched as streets filled up with water. I've watched trees falling, one after the other, in the vacant lot across the street from my home. I've watched surf hitting buildings and roads far from the ocean. Storms are a part of east coast life.

And, in *Shadows on a Cape Cod Wedding* the wedding is a bit damp, but it does take place … everybody …well, almost everybody … lives happily ever after when the storm clears.

Which should be what happens in a mystery. And in life.

Why I Love/Hate My Computer

During the past week my computer has given me nightmares.

Now, I'm usually a fairly calm person. Go ahead – ask my husband. Ask my children. Well – no – don't ask my children about when they were in high school. And don't ask my husband about when I'm under a deadline. But, other than that, I'm usually very restrained. Accepting. I take deep breaths. I would have been great in World War II Britain. (The "Keep Calm and Carry On" years.)

And after years of writing (corporate, theoretically nonfiction,) before I'd written one word of fiction or entered the world of publishing, I'd honed the ability to smile through dozens of political rewrites, knew the joy of collating at three a.m., understood the rationale for squirreling away pounds of carbon and gallons of Wite-out so I would never, ever, run out, and was known as one of the few who could convince a weary secretary to retype a page one more time because a comma needed to be added.

When electric typewriters became common, I loved my Selectric. When they turned into electric typewriters with memory, I was in heaven. And my office had one of the first computers that could process words and make sense of them.

No doubt: I love my computer. Every day I spend eight to twelve hours a day with my keyboard and mouse and screen, writing, researching, sending and receiving e-mails, blogging, Facebooking. In short, being an author.

Until last week, when my world came crashing down.

My computer was, I will admit, getting a little on in years. It groaned a little. It hesitated. It stopped and started. (Much as I do some mornings.) It would no longer play videos. It wouldn't accept updates. I started to worry. Yes, I backed up my manuscripts "in the cloud." But those clouds have looked pretty dark recently. And I have a book deadline looming. So one morning I woke up and decided it was time. Even computers come to an end.

I ruthlessly pulled out cables and drove my old tower to Best Buy. Where, I discovered, few people use desk top computers anymore. It's all laptops. Well, my study is set up for a desktop, and I wasn't ready to give that up, so a very patient and polite young Geek (they are actually called that at Best Buy) explained that I could, indeed, buy another tower. But then he introduced me to all-in-ones, and I fell hard.

If any of you are as far behind the times as I was, an "all-in-one" is basically Spanx for your computer hardware. It squishes everything except your mouse and keyboard into a flat screen – a glorious flat screen, which includes a camera that won't fall off the top of the screen, speakers that won't take up desk space – and no pedestal at all. It was gorgeous. And the Geek promised to personally transfer all my files — emails, mailing list, and, of course, all my manuscripts — into this wonderful new computer. (For a not-so-small fee, of course.) And he'd update my Windows. And my Mail. Everything as Up-to-Date as Kansas City before any tornadoes.

I was wooed and won. I handed him my credit card and my tower and went home to clean my desk to prepare for the coming of the new computer.

Two days later it was in my study. Six hours after that I was beginning to figure out how to find mail on it. Maybe. Then I tried to find my mailing list – an essential piece of my business. But that file was (my stomach disappeared to somewhere south of the cellar) empty. I dialed the 800 number the Geek had given me. Another nice Geek told me to attach the backup files I was given to the computer. All would be well.

An hour later? All was not well.

I called the local store. I took the pretty new computer back. I was assured by Geek One that he would resolve the problem. Just a matter of consolidating files. Not a problem for him! I had to go to Portland for a couple of hours? Stop on my way home.

I did. The computer was "almost ready." Not to worry. He'd call.

He didn't. Until the next afternoon. Seems my software for the mailing list didn't work with the fancy new Word system. But never fear! He was trying to get through to the software company. He'd make it work!

He called again the next afternoon. He had the fix. Not to worry! (At this point I hadn't had a computer for … but who was counting days? I was counting hours! Cut off from the world! No email! No Facebook! No new pages written!)

And, by the way, he asked, what was my password for my mailing list?

"No password," I said. "I never gave it a password. I'm the only one who uses it."

"It needs a password to open it," he said. "I can't fix it without a password."

"No password," I said.

"I'll see," he answered. "Don't worry."

He hung up. I worried.

Two days later, I got another call. A recording. My computer was ready!

I wasn't sure I believed it. All night I wondered what "ready" meant. "Ready" to throw out? "Ready" without my ten years of mailing list?

When I arrived at the store, Geek One showed me how it all worked. He told me I might have some problems. He also assured me that the next time I bought a new computer I'd have the same issues with the mailing list again. He smiled. I smiled. I took the computer home.

I can now report that the mailing list software works beautifully. I'm much relieved about that.

But this afternoon a fellow writer sent me pictures and a guest essay for today's Maine Crime Writers blog. I can't figure out how to move the pictures she sent me into files so I can upload them into the blog.

Today I was also asked to send an edited chapter of my latest book to a magazine so they could excerpt it.

I ended up retyping the whole chapter.

I haven't quite mastered Windows 8 yet.

But, never fear. A copy of Windows 8 for Dummies will arrive tomorrow.

Editing? One Dozen
Points to Check

I'm an author, but I have a confession. I really don't like writing.

Now, that doesn't mean never, and it doesn't mean I'm going to stop.

It means that for me, the most difficult and frustrating part of writing a book is sitting (ass-in-chair) and grinding out the first draft. Assuming that life doesn't always allow for writing time every day (there is that laundry, and those appearances and all those holidays) and that an average adult mystery has 75,000-80,000 words, that's a lot of sitting and stressing time.

On a first draft I try to write 7-10 pages a day. Some days I do more; some less.

My reward? Editing. I *love* editing. It's like smoothing the edges of a sculpture, or rounding out the depth of a hole, or adding just the right spice to the soup.

Right now I'm editing a manuscript that was rejected several time. It has a fast plot and interesting characters, but I've realized it needed a different voice. And more layering. I'm happily in the depth of editing right now, wondering why I didn't see those problems before.

So how do I edit? I read first for plot; second for character; third for facts; fourth for rhythm; and fifth for grammar and spelling. Then I read for plot again.

Here are a dozen things (big and little) that I check for.

1. Character names. Make them easy to pronounce. And no characters should have names that sound alike, or that start with the same first letter of the alphabet.

2. Time lines: List the dates/days covered by the manuscript (including backstory if necessary) and confirm that all the characters can be – and are - where they're supposed to be given that time frame. That an eight-year-old wasn't alive when the World Trade Center was attacked. That I haven't skipped days. And this is a good time to check weather, too. Consistency is vital. It can rain on a sunny day, but if it does, there should be a reason for it to rain. And maybe there'll be a rainbow. Have I set the book at the right time of year? Does geography or weather influence the plot? (If it's there – it should.)

3. Voice, Tone and Point-of view. Is there one voice? Two? Is the voice you've chosen the best one to tell the story? Is there any "head hopping" between characters? Can the reader identify

characters by the way they speak? They shouldn't all sound the same. (Rhythm is important here.)

4. How many layers are there in the story? The obvious one (e.g. solving the mystery; finding the treasure) is one. But what personal relationship development is there? What have the main characters learned about themselves? Is there a theme to the book as a whole? Can anything be added to flesh this theme out?

5. How does the manuscript look on a page? Are there too many long paragraphs? Too much unattributed dialogue?

6. Search out and kill repeated words. Use new ways to say what has to be said. Eliminate words like "there" and "things" and those words (all authors have them) that are used too often. (Two of my personal over-used words are "just" and "really.")

7. Look for adjectives and adverbs, too. Adverbs should be used only on rare occasions. Kill them, or replace them with action verbs. Kill long descriptions and strings of adjectives.

8. Edit the manuscript on the screen. Then print it out, take a red pencil to the pages, and input those edits. The print it out again, and this time read it all (yes – all of it) out loud. Amazing what changes I'll make while reading the words out loud.

9. Fact check. Historical facts, sure. But also little things. If the hero hates squash in chapter five, he shouldn't order it for dinner in chapter thirty-seven. Check food. Clothing. Do they reflect each character's choices? Why? If there isn't a reason for the heroine to wear a purple dress, then why mention it? If I'm poisoning someone, how does the poison taste? (Yes; I've tasted the ones in my books.) If something tastes awful, would it be credible for the victim to eat/drink it?

10. Timing. Action keeps people reading. But a book can't be a series of car chases. (Pretty boring.) And even if the book isn't a mystery, tension should be throughout the book — in actions, in dialogue, in relationships, in anticipation.

11. Secrets. Everyone has a secret, right? So should every character. The reader may never know all of them. But I should. And if secrets are revealed … to whom? Why? How does that change the dynamics of relationships? Actions?

12. Point to the Hole. Is there any part of your plot that is logically questionable? Any special knowledge the heroine has to have acquired? Feature these before they come up in the plot. Your hero learned martial arts as a child. The heroine speaks Spanish because she was an exchange student. Uncle Max loved to collect books with leather bindings, but couldn't read

small print. That's why the secret map was found in one of his books, and he didn't know it was there.

13. First page, first chapter. It may be all the agent/editor/reader actually reads. Make it sing, full of action, not backstory or weather.

14. Chapter endings. Are there cliffhangers? Questions? What at the end of each chapter will make the reader want to turn the page?

The changes made while editing may seem small, but they're what will make the manuscript sing.

And the editor buy. And readers read.

Bringing People (Back) to Life

Because the books I write set in nineteenth century Maine are full of real people, most of whom lived in the small town of Wiscasset, I'm often asked, "How do you write about real people?"

In most of my books, my main characters and their families are fictional, but the minor characters really lived and worked in Wiscasset in the years I set my stories. I focus on the everyday life of children, women and ordinary men. I once wrote that George Washington would never ride through one of my books.

But now I've broken that self-imposed rule, three times.

In *Uncertain Glory* two of my major characters are boys who really did publish the town's newspaper in the mid-nineteenth century. In *Shadows of a Down East Summer* I brought artist Winslow Homer back to life. And in *Contrary Winds*, an unpublished book I wrote set in 1777, part of the action is at the Battles of Saratoga, and yes, several generals do ride through my pages. (But not George Washington.)

I loved the challenge of writing a story around the

facts. For example, when I wrote about Winslow Homer I focused on his life in the summer of 1890. What was his daily schedule? Where did he live? What did he paint? Who was he surrounded by? I didn't change anything about him. But my fictional characters in that book borrowed the identities of two young Maine women who posed for him that summer. (I apologized to the actual women in my acknowledgements.)

In *Uncertain Glory*, the major characters are also real people. Not as well-known as Winslow Homer, certainly, but one became a major figure in nineteenth century Maine newspaper publishing, and another became an author of adventure stories for boys.

Joseph Wood came from the small town of Wiscasset, where he published his first newspaper, a weekly called the *Wiscasset Herald*, for almost a year when he was a teenager. Later, after apprenticing a few years in Portland, he returned to Wiscasset and published the *Seaside Oracle* from 1869-1876. After that he published newspapers in Bath, Skowhegan, and Bar Harbor. He remained involved with Maine newspapers until he died in 1923. The idea of a teenaged boy who published a town newspaper intrigued me. I wanted to share his story.

But I needed more. Joe Wood actually published his newspaper in 1859. I set my first draft of *Uncertain Glory* then, in the dead of winter, when ice and snow were daily challenges. I added Nell, a twelve-year-old girl spiritualist. Her character is fictional, but based on the lives of several well-known spiritualists of that period.

But the story was still too thin. I put the manuscript aside for several years, but it was always in the back of my mind. Then, checking dates for another project, I realized that 1859 was close to 1861. (Sometimes I'm really focused …!)

How much more exciting would it be if Joe not only had personal issues, but also was trying to cover the beginning of the Civil War in his newspaper?

I hesitated a little, but then remembered what one of my editors had once told me when I was similarly stuck on a point of history versus fiction. She reminded me I was writing historical **fiction**.

I researched what was happening in Maine in April of 1861, and was thrilled to discover a group of letters that described events in Wiscasset, Joe's home town.

I added another character: Owen, a nine-year-old African-American boy who helped Joe at the newspaper, and I modified the role of Joe's (real) friend Charlie Farrar. Finally, I was ready to write my story.

So Joe and Charlie are actual people, as are many of the minor characters in *Uncertain Glory*. Nell and Owen are fictional, but based on people who lived in 1861. And Joe really published his paper in 1859. I cover all of that in my historical notes to *Uncertain Glory*.

I changed the year. I didn't change the personalities of the characters, or what they did, or what was happening in the nation or the state.

And, yes: it is historical **fiction**.

In *Contrary Winds* I stuck close to the dates events

happened both in Maine and in Saratoga, and what happened during those events. But the characters who lived through those events are fictional, much as Winslow Homer was a real person, but I added some logical but fictional people around him in *Shadows on a Down East Summer*.

The most important part of writing historical fiction which includes actual people is to get them right. Not to have them do things they didn't do; not to have them dream twentieth or twenty-first century dreams. Not to put them in places they weren't. They must be grounded in their period.

Fictional characters must be grounded in the world in which they live, but you can move them around, and give them different experiences.

Not so with an actual person.

We can't change history.

Mystery Conferences

I'm writing this in Bethesda, Maryland, where most attendees of Malice Domestic, the annual mystery conference featuring "cozy," or "traditional" mysteries, will arrive today. More than one hundred and fifty authors will be here, along with five or six hundred fans.

A couple of weeks ago I also attended a one-day mystery conference (Maine Crime Wave) in Portland, Maine. It was small, as mystery conferences go — about eighty people. And everyone I spoke with was an aspiring or published author of mysteries.

Two very different sorts of conferences.

I won't even start to list the number of mystery conferences held every year, ranging from the granddaddy of them all, Bouchercon, which attracts writers of all mystery genres and several thousand fans, down to the Maine Crime Wave.

Why attend a mystery conference?

Some conferences, like the Maine Crime Wave in Portland, and Sleuthfest (in Florida) are aimed at writers. Workshops and talks are about writing techniques; marketing; the state of the industry; and often agents and editors are in attendance. Other conferences, like Bouchercon and Malice Domestic and Left Coast Crime (and many more,) are aimed at readers. Panels feature published writers talking on topics such as "The weirdest thing I've done in the name of research"; "Why are so many crime novels set in New England?"; "What happens when weather interferes with solving a crime?" and so forth. Most of them are fun topics, and give the authors on the panels a chance to plug their books. Some conferences, like Crime Bake (in Massachusetts in November) try to appeal to both readers and writers.

I attended my first mystery conference as a "pre-published" author. I was looking for an agent. (I didn't find one there.) It was a two-day conference in Philadelphia, and I only attended one day. I learned a lot, and loved the idea of a whole room full of people (all of whom knew a lot more about mysteries than I did) discussing serial killer fiction and cozies and who the up-and-coming authors were. I went home exhausted, but intrigued. I had my first inkling of how much I had to learn.

My next conference was Malice Domestic several years later, and I attended it with excitement as a first-time Agatha Award nominee. (Did I mention some conferences give out coveted awards?)

Yes, I was overwhelmed. But being a nominee, I was a part of everything. I didn't exactly feel at home, but I did feel as though I belonged. I had a role to play.

Since then I've attended mystery conferences all over

the United States… an average of two or three each year, which is a small number. I know authors who attend ten or twelve each year. Every year.

Attending a conference takes time away from writing, costs money, and the number of books sold at each conference doesn't justify the trip. What does justify the expense is meeting fans, connecting with booksellers, hobnobbing with other authors (and agents and editors,) and getting out into the world and away from your computer screen.

If you're thinking of signing up for a mystery conference, here are some basic hints:

1. Decide if you're interested in a fan conference or a conference on writing. They're not the same.

2. If you're published, register early and try to get on a panel so you and your book(s) can be showcased. This will also mean your books will be carried in the conference book room and you can do a signing.

3. If you have (and authors should have) bookmarks, postcards, pins, brochures … anything that markets your books … bring multi-copies. Authors cover designated tables with giveaways. And attendees load up!

4. Even if you're on a panel, double-check with one or more of the bookstores that will be at the

conference to make sure they'll order and bring copies of your latest book.

5. Attend as many panels/talks/events at the conference as you can. But if you're exhausted, sitting at the bar (even if you drink coffee) is not a bad idea. Friendships and book deals are made at conference bars.

6. Don't be shy. Introduce yourself to people sitting or standing next to you. After all, you already have mysteries in common. And if your favorite author is there, be sure to tell him or her how much you love their books! (Authors never get tired of hearing that.)

7. If you're a fan, look at the conference website for the list of attending authors, and bring copies of their books you already own to be signed. Yes, the booksellers at the conference will tell you it's better to buy the books on site ... but few authors will object to signing a book bought elsewhere.

8. Wear comfortable shoes. You'll be walking and standing a lot and (except for some awards dinners) mystery conferences are casual.

9. Don't worry about acquiring too many books. (Is there such a thing?) Most conferences have contracted with a shipper so you can have your new signed books (or dirty laundry) shipped home for you.

10. Be sure to take a notebook. You're going to hear about new authors, new books, or maybe get a great new plot twist for the book you're writing. You don't want to forget anything. And you'll be exhausted at the end of two or three days. Take my word for it.

11. Worried about the expense? If you're a member of Sisters in Crime and/or Mystery Writers of America (and you should be,) post what would help. Do you need a ride to or from the conference? To or from the airport? Would you like to share a room at the conference hotel? (Try to stay where the action is … it may be cheaper to stay at another hotel, but you'll miss having a room to escape to if you need to take a deep breath. Or drop off books. Or collapse after the banquet. Or just need a bathroom without a long line.)

12. Don't forget to enjoy the experience!

Dialogue …. It's What Keeps the Story (And My Life) Moving

When I was fourteen, someone (I honestly don't remember who) took me to see a play at the Boothbay Playhouse, a summer equity company in Boothbay, Maine. I loved it. And I wrote a fan letter to the leading actress, Harryetta Peterka.

To my surprise (and, I think, my mother's embarrassment,) Harryetta shared the note with the two producers at the theatre, and one of them, Jim Wilmot, called and asked me if I'd like to usher there. I wouldn't get paid, would work one evening a week, and would get to see the show for free.

I immediately agreed, and when I discovered that an older boy in my neighborhood who had a license and a pickup truck worked there parking cars, I asked Jim if I could usher all five nights the theatre was open each week. I had a ride. And so, for the rest of the summer, I ushered every night, and stood behind the last row in the balcony to listen to every word of every play.

The next summer Jim made me head usher. I still

didn't get paid, but I called potential ushers and scheduled them, worked every night, and, when intermissions got busy, I sold candy and sodas and coffee, too. The year after that I worked during the day at the *Boothbay Register*, the local weekly newspaper, but five nights a week you could find me at the Playhouse. Ushering, and listening. And so it continued.

The year after my stint at the newspaper I worked full time (and was paid! thirty dollars a week) during the day at the Playhouse's ticket booth in Boothbay Harbor, and then got to the Playhouse in time to, of course, usher every night.

After that summer I graduated from ushering. I worked at the Playhouse box office. But I stayed every night until every play was over. And working at the Playhouse itself I heard many more lines, many times. The hard-working New York repertory company was performing one play while they were rehearsing a second and learning the lines to a third. They produced nine plays each summer, from Ibsen to Ionesco to Noel Coward to Neil Simon to Thornton Wilder.

All day, every day, I heard dialogue. I learned many of the plays by heart, without trying. I learned which lines got laughs or gasps, and which didn't.

I didn't realize it, but I was learning to write dialogue.

I wrote my first play when I was in high school. When I went to college, my years at the Playhouse (which continued summers) encouraged me to major in drama as well as English. I wrote plays for children's theatre as part of my senior thesis. And then I graduated and looked for a job.

After a number of interviews, as luck would have it, I was interviewed by a public relations manager at AT&T who'd attended the Yale School of Drama. He asked me if I had any of my plays with me. A young graduate, just twenty-one, of course I had writing samples. I handed him one of my plays — I think it was about a chipmunk and an owl. (Unlikely though that was.)

He sat at his imposing mahogany desk and read several pages. Then he handed my play back to me and said, "You can write dialogue."

"Yes," I agreed.

"Then you can write executive speeches," he pronounced. (I hadn't even realized anyone but the President of the United States had a speechwriter.)

I was hired. My first speech was for the president of the Western Electric Company – then the manufacturing and supply arm of the Bell System. I was the first management woman in their public relations department. I wrote speeches, videos, films. articles, and went on to directing, producing, writing and "staring" in a daily television program for AT&T employees.

In 1998, many jobs after that, I left AT&T, but I haven't stopped writing. I still depend on dialogue to move my stories along.

And, yes, it all started with a fan letter I wrote when I was fourteen, which led to a summer job, which changed what I majored in at college, which led to a corporate career.

I still smile whenever a reviewer praises my dialogue.

Yes, I can write dialogue. I've been doing it since high school.

Marketing and Competitive Research Before You Write? Oh, Yes.

My new mystery series (Mainely Needlepoint) has just debuted with *Twisted Threads*. Publishing being what it is, I've already finished the second book in the series (*Threads of Evidence*), which is in the middle of copy edits. *Thread and Gone*, the third manuscript, is due in about a month. One of the largest challenges of writing and publishing is keeping ahead of readers!

Many people have asked me "why needlepoint?" As some asked last spring, when *Uncertain Glory*, my most recent historical (set during the first two weeks of the Civil War) was published, "How did you choose that time period?"

The answer to both questions is "competitive research and marketing." Although the idea of sitting down and writing what is in your heart (or mind) sounds wonderful, in truth, writing without research can lead a writer down a path to manuscript rejection.

What kind of research would you do for a book that isn't even written?

Publishers want to know what the competition for your books will be, and how many people will be interested in buying it. A growing number of publishers (like mine) want to see the numbers before they sign onto a new book, or series.

But, don't panic. Sometimes the research is relatively simple.

My publisher for *Uncertain Glory* was enticed by the Civil War timing of the book — even though the book was set in Maine, far from the 1861 front. Reason? The book would be published during the 150th anniversary of the war, when people would be thinking about 1861-1864. It's a period covered in most schools in grades four through eight, the right age for my young readers, and for teachers and librarians to add to their collections.

Three of the book's major characters are boys. (Conventional wisdom says few boys will read a book with a girl as a major character; girls will read books about boys or girls.) I'd also checked the title. *Uncertain Glory* is taken from Shakespeare ("the uncertain glory of an April day") and it had only been used as a title for one nonfiction book and an early Errol Flynn movie. Although titles can't be copyrighted, it's not great to have a dozen books in print that could be confused with yours. In my proposal to the publisher I also included an annotated list of other books for young people set during this period, and why *Uncertain Glory* would be different. And, of course, better.

Okay. But what about a mystery? How would you do market research for one of those?

Funny you should ask. Because the publisher of my Mainely Needlepoint series wanted competitive analysis/market research done as part of my first proposal. (They also wanted summaries of the first three books in the series, fifty pages of the first book and the reasons why I would be the best person to write the series.) I believe my market research tipped the scale in my favor.

I wanted to write a traditional, cozy, mystery series with a little edge. I knew cozies with "craft" backgrounds were popular, so I looked at what was already being published. I wouldn't have wanted to suggest, say, a series with a background of beading, to a publisher that already had one. Or a series about quilt shops when several were already being published.

How did I find out who was publishing what, and how successful they were? The answers were simple to find. We're lucky today to have Amazon and BN.com. Search for "beading mysteries" on those sites and you'll have a good start on research. In my case I found one other needlepoint series, an embroidery series, a machine embroidery series, and five knitting or crochet series, all of which I included in my analysis since I suspected they shared some of the same readers.

I then looked to see how many books were in each series; whether the series was still being published; what their publishers were; and whether they were mass market originals, hard cover originals, or trade paper originals.

After reading one or two books in each current successful series it was clear needlepoint would be a good topic: of the three series featuring embroidery, even the one listed as a Needlecraft Mystery included other forms of stitchery.

But how could I make my series stand out?

All the craft mysteries I'd looked at were set in embroidery/needlecraft/yarn shops, and all but one of the protagonists owned such a shop. I looked at geographic locations, too: only one series was set in New England.

I decided to set my series in Maine (a plus because many readers know me as a Maine author,) to have my series connected to a custom needlepoint business run by a young woman with a past and her grandmother, allowing for plots involving people of different ages. And since my earlier series was set in the antiques world, my Mainely Needlepoint series would build on that. My needlepointers would also identify and restore antique needlepoint. (More story ideas …)

But how many readers were interested in needlepoint? A little googling told me. Needlepoint is a popular craft, especially among middle-aged and older women … and men. Women over forty are also the largest readers of traditional mysteries. But I still needed numbers. Publishers want numbers.

The American Needlepoint Guild has 164 chapters, 9500 members, an on-line presence and a bimonthly magazine. The National Needle Arts Association is the professional organization connecting the 873 retail shops and 256 wholesalers of crafts/yarn. Two magazines and several national conventions each year reach needlepointers. Needlepoint is also popular in the UK and in Canada.

Result of that research? A three-book contract, and suggestions of several specific ways to reach readers who might be interested in a needlepoint series. My agent told me he liked the marketing plan so much, if it hadn't sold to one publisher, he was prepared to market it to other editors.

(Note: he didn't mention the plots of the first three books in the series, or my writing style.)

It took me about two weeks to research and write the proposal for the series. And not only did it help my editor make a decision, it also helped me develop the background for the series, and its characters.

Right now I'm busy promoting *Twisted Threads* and writing the third in the series. *Threads of Evidence*, the second in the series, will be published in August of this year.

I'm not focusing on writing another series: two is plenty for now! But I do have several other ideas. And, before those ideas get too far along, I'll be doing some market research.

It just makes business sense.

Making the Next Deadline

Right now I'm writing or editing eight to ten hours or more a day. No – that isn't my preferred way of writing, although I'll admit it does focus me. Why am I doing it, then? I have a September first deadline for my next book, and circumstances beyond my control (health, family, technology failures, speaking commitments … the usual list) conspired to push me into this corner.

Seven weeks away from a deadline I've usually finished several drafts of a book and am working on "final" edits.

This time around I've written (and edited — my style is to edit as I go, so my first draft is pretty polished) about sixty percent of what will be the final version. I'm not happy with it yet, though, so I keep editing what I've written. Each day I edit out perhaps four pages and add five. A slow way to go.

Two of my writing friends also have September 1 deadlines. I haven't seen either of them recently, for obvious reasons, but we do occasionally exchange panicked emails. One finished her book in April, but the subject matter expert to whom she gave the manuscript to fact check told her the plot wouldn't work. Despite her research, she'd gotten a couple of key points wrong. The legal world would laugh and her character would be disbarred. A big oops. She's totally rewriting her book.

My other friend has had major family issues. She couldn't race from bedside to bedside and concentrate on a plot, so the plot didn't come together. Now she has seven weeks to make sure it does. Yet the family issues continue. She's beginning to whisper words like, "extension?"

I'm not. I'll make my deadline. I'm writing this blog surrounded by the tools of an author's trade. A list of characters. Time lines. Character bios. Genealogy charts. Notes from previous books in my series to make sure I don't change any places or characters who've appeared before. Notes from my favorite book on writing, Donald Maass' *The Fire in Fiction,* reminding me about micro tension in dialogue. Lists of scenes. Lists of words to describe weather at the time of year the book is set. Lists of animals and birds, ditto. A side list of questions to be researched that I'll have to fill in (later today? tomorrow? there's not much time.) A running analysis of chapter lengths. (Currently they range from three pages to twenty. Hmm. I'll need to look at that.) Notes on prints I'll choose to be in chapter headings, since this is a Shadows Antique Print Mystery. Adding the headings is the last thing I do before sending a book in, but it can take days, so if I can get a little ahead on it, that's good. At this stage, every hour counts.

My back aches. My tendency to migraines is challenged

several times a week. My husband, who's trying not to complain, is doing all the errands and the cooking. What bothers him most is that even when I emerge from my second floor study I'm not always "myself." Believe me. I love him, and the support he's giving me.

But my head's still in my manuscript, rearranging scenes, thinking up deeper motivations, adding new clues or complications.

My manuscript will be finished by September 1.

But I'm afraid I'll miss this summer.

Some Thoughts on the
Mystery Series

I write two mystery series; so far, seven books in the Shadows Antique Print series and three in the Mainely Needlepoint series.

I'm well aware that compared with masters of the series like Sue Grafton, Susan Wittig Albert, Dana Stabenow, Sarah Graves, Anne Perry, and so many more whose lists of series titles number in the twenties or above, my paltry "ten" ranks me as a beginner in the field, though, so I'm always interested in learning more about how people see the mystery series and its characters.

Recently that topic seems to be on other peoples' minds, too.

Those who write mysteries set in small towns often joke about having to "avoid the dreaded Cabot Cove syndrome." Simply put, if your series runs long enough, and you don't bring in enough strangers, eventually you'll kill off everyone in town.

This month's *Down East*, a Maine magazine edited by Paul Doiron, friend and acclaimed mystery writer himself, tackled the issue directly. It reported that in Honduras, the country with the highest annual murder rate in the world (who knew?) there are 86 murders for every 100,000 people. In Cabot Cove, Maine, the setting for *Murder, She Wrote*, the annual murder rate was 149 per 100,000. (Not counting re-runs.) (I wonder who on *Down East's* staff had the job of counting.)

After reading that, I spent the past weekend at Crime Bake, a wonderful mystery conference held annually in Massachusetts, hosted by the New England branches of Mystery Writers of America and Sisters in Crime, and one I definitely recommend to any mystery writer or fan. Discussions about the series came up several times, in panels, and in side conversations among attendees.

Agents, editors, booksellers and fans all agreed they loved a good series. They sold well and were predictable: they were the bread and butter of the mystery world. Authors also loved the two or three book contracts most series authors were getting, even if there were some downsides to committing time and money years in advance.

Most authors talked about the character and plot development needed to keep a series interesting; to keep a "story arc" going throughout a series of books. Others pointed at authors like Lee Child who never changed their protagonist from book to book, ensuring that their readers got the same person every time. Clearly, that works for him.

Fans recalled authors who "killed off" their favorite

characters. Some could forgive; some refused to go back to the series, or, indeed, to any other book by the same author. Those readers were a minority of fans, but a vocal one.

Authors whose series were discontinued by their publishers before their characters' story arc had been completed talked of ways to finish the story, for themselves and their fans. Some had written short stories or e-book novellas to tie up loose ends. Roberta Isleib had one of the most creative solutions. The protagonist in her first series, a professional golfer, was left debating whether or not she was going to marry when her series was discontinued. In Roberta's next series, she had her new protagonist, a professional in a totally different field, turn on the sports news and see a large sparkling engagement ring on the golfer's finger. Story arc completed.

Perhaps what was most important, though, was that everyone at the conference was taking the subject so very seriously. The basic issue was keeping readers (and the writer) interested throughout a series. Most people agreed the protagonist was more important than the plot of the individual mystery. It was the protagonist, and the characters surrounding the protagonist who re-appeared in each book in the series, who pulled readers in and convinced them to buy another book in the series. The background of their lives, the way they lived those lives, and their relationships with each other, were much more important than the particular mystery presented and solved in each book.

People read for character; not plot. I heard it over and over, throughout the conference. Something to think about as I flesh out my next books. Because I have some interesting characters I'd like you to meet.

When the Editor Says
Changes Must Be Made

I just returned from a book festival in New York State, weary after meeting and greeting and driving many miles to do so. My husband welcomed me home with a hug, a glass of wine, and the words, "It's here."

I knew exactly what he meant. My next couple of weeks have just been preempted by the manuscript I finished six weeks ago. The mystery I hope you'll be reading next March.

My editor's been studying it line by line for the past month, and now it's winged back to me to fix the major and minor mistakes she's found, eliminate the dull spots she located, and add in a tense moment or twelve that I've thought of in the meantime.

I haven't looked at the red-penciled pages yet, but I'm sure she's made improvements I agree with on almost every page. I'll look at her marks and groan, wondering how I could have made such stupid mistakes, or written so awkwardly. Some of her comments I'll disagree with. Some sections of the book I'll re-write completely, either based on her suggestions, my own inspiration, or a combination of both.

Both my editor and I want the manuscript to be as strong as it can be, and at this point it's a joint venture. I welcome improvements.

I've had editors in the past who made almost no comments. I've also had editors who only made very large, overall, comments. Once a mystery editor felt I'd made an "inappropriate individual" the killer. Sure, I'd explained why he'd done the deed. Of course, I had red herrings, and other suspects. But she just didn't like that he was the guilty one. If she was going to publish the book, I'd have to make the killer someone else. I added in another character, starting in Chapter 1, and wove that character all through the book, leaving everything else pretty much the same. It was an interesting exercise. Strengthened the book, too, because it added one more suspect.

Another editor looked at my manuscripts with smaller vision. She had almost a phobia about commas. She went through my manuscript, every time, and took 95% of my commas out. The first time I had a small fit. I'm not in love with commas, but when I put one in, it's for a reason. But The Great Comma Elimination was clearly not up for discussion.

I found myself wonderfully vindicated when, after all other editing was finished, the copy editor went through and put all my necessary commas back in. After that I didn't question any eliminated commas on the first editing rounds. I just made sure I had the same copy editor.

My most frustrating experience with an editor was with one of my children's books. The editor decided the book was too long, and said the first fifty pages must be cut. Totally. I fought that one. Hard. But it was no use. My problem was, of course, that a lot had happened in those fifty pages. By cutting fifty pages I had to cut several characters, and what I felt was important depth to the main character's back story, which was now being "told" instead of "shown." The cut pages also eliminated an entire geographic location which I'd hoped to include for historical reasons. Gone. None of the "compare and contrast" I'd hope the book would illustrate. The book is a strong one, but I still feel those first pages would have added a depth it never regained.

(Now years later I've gotten my revenge, of sorts. I just re-edited and e-published those pages as *The Charleston Hurricane of 1804*, a prequel to my *Seaward Born*.)

When I speak to groups I'm often asked if I'm hurt by editors' changes. (I'm seldom asked if those changes improve my books.) Do if I agree with the changes editors ask for? Usually I do. Hey — the boss is usually right!

But there have been times when the editor(s) have not been right, and, yes, those times I've stood firm. The time an editor suggested I change a reference to Monhegan Island to "a real island." Or when I described a Maine blizzard in 1838 in which "drifts were above the heads of the younger school children." An editor wrote in the margin, "Snow doesn't get this high." After due thought I wrote back, "In 1838 Maine it did." The line stayed.

Directions to places in Maine have sometimes been questioned. (Yes, they were traveling east – not north.) One editor pointed out helpfully that a woman in one of my historicals was always wearing a blue dress. I'd forgotten to describe different clothing? No, I wrote back. She only had one dress. (But I added a few words to make sure other readers would understand that, too.)

I'm a firm believer in critique groups, in critical "first readers" (mine is my husband,) in agents who give feedback, and in editors. Having a manuscript published without first having someone evaluating it dispassionately and pointing out its weaknesses would be like a woman dressing in her best, applying makeup and combing her hair — and never looking in a full-length mirror before she went out into the world.

Today I'm unpacking, writing this blog, catching up with other paperwork, and looking forward to tomorrow, when I'll open that envelope from my editor, and begin again to make that book the best it can be.

I owe it to myself and to my readers, and I'm lucky to have an editor who believes my book and its readers are worth her time, too.

Lea Wait

writes the Agatha-finalist Shadows Antique Print Mystery series, the Mainely Needlepoint series, and historical novels for young people. She lives with her husband, artist Bob Thomas, and their black cat, Shadow, in a house built in 1774 on the coast of Maine. Before she married Bob she worked in public relations and strategic planning at AT&T and adopted her four daughters, who were born in Thailand, Korea, Hong Kong and India. A fourth generation antique dealer, Lea was also an antique print dealer for many years. Now she writes full-time. She invites you to friend her on Facebook and Goodreads, to check her website, www.leawait.com for more information about her and her books, and to read the blog she writes with other Maine mystery authors, www.mainecrimewriters.com. And if you enjoyed this book, she'd love you to post a review on one of the on-line booksellers' sites or on Goodreads.

Books by Lea Wait

Shadows Antique Print Mysteries
Shadows at the Fair (1)
Shadows on the Coast of Maine (2)
Shadows on the Ivy (3)
Shadows at the Spring Show (4)
Shadows of a Down East Summer (5)
Shadows on a Cape Cod Wedding (6)
Shadows on a Maine Christmas (7)
Shadows on a Morning in Maine (8)

Mainely Needlepoint Series
Twisted Threads (1)
Threads of Evidence (2)
Thread and Gone (3)

Historicals for ages 8 and up
Stopping to Home
Seaward Born
Wintering Well
Finest Kind
Uncertain Glory

CPSIA information can be obtained
at www.ICGtesting.com
Printed in the USA
BVHW040944170420
577808BV00010B/1309